On Racism, Religion and Reconciliation

Contemplation
of
Imam W. Deen Mohammed

Edited by Ronald B. Shaheed

2

Sincere gratitude to Dr. Nasir Ahmad for his tireless work in transcribing and editing the digital material from which this publication was compiled. May Allah (G_d) continue to bless him with the best of health and spirit.

Edited and published by Ronald B. Shaheed
2017

ISBN: 978-0-692-98330-0

Contents

Preface

Dr. Carter G. Woodson, historian and father of Black History Month, in his book, *The Miseducation of the Negro*,[1] said, "If you can control a man's thinking you do not have to worry about his action. When you determine what a man shall think you do not have to concern yourself about what he will do. If you make a man feel that he is inferior, you do not have to compel him to accept an inferior status, for he will seek it himself. If you make a man think that he is justly an outcast, you do not have to order him to the back door. He will go without being told; and if there is no back door, his very nature will demand one." He also said, "As another has well said, to handicap a student by teaching him that his black face is a curse and that his struggle to change his condition is hopeless is the worst sort of lynching." Well-known scholar and intellectual, W.E.B. Dubois, in his book, *The Souls of Black Folk*,[2] said, "The Problem of the twentieth century is the problem of the color-line, the relation of the darker to the lighter races of men in Asia and Africa, in America and the islands of the sea."

Ida B. Wells,[3] journalist, newspaper editor, civil rights leader and one of the founders of the NAACP stated that, "The lesson this teaches and which every Afro-American should ponder well, is that a Winchester rifle should have a place of honor in every black home, and it should be used for that protection which the law refuses to give. When the white man who is always the aggressor knows he runs as great a risk of biting the dust every time his Afro-American victim does, he will have greater respect for Afro-American life. The more the Afro-American yields and cringes and begs, the more he has to do so, the more he is insulted, outraged and lynched."

In his autobiography, *Up from Slavery*,[4] Booker T. Washington, said, "I pity from the bottom of my heart any nation or body of people that is so unfortunate as to get entangled in the net of slavery. I have long since ceased to cherish any spirit of bitterness against the Southern white people on account of the enslavement of my race. No one section of our country was wholly responsible for its introduction, and, besides, it was recognized and protected for years by the General Government. Having once got its tentacles fastened on to the economic and social life of the Republic, it was no easy matter for the country to relieve itself of the institution. Then, when we rid ourselves of prejudice, or racial feeling, and look facts in the face, we must acknowledge that, notwithstanding the cruelty and moral wrong of slavery, the ten million Negroes inhabiting this country, who themselves or whose ancestors went through the school of American slavery, are in a stronger and more hopeful condition, materially, intellectually, morally, and religiously, than is true of an equal number of black people in any other portion of the globe. This is so to such an extent that Negroes in this country, who themselves or whose forefathers went through the school of slavery, are constantly returning to Africa as missionaries to enlighten those who remained in the fatherland. This I say, not to justify slavery (On the other hand, I condemn it as an institution, as we all know that in America it was established for selfish and financial reasons, and not from a missionary motive), but to call attention to a fact, and to show how Providence so often uses men and institutions to accomplish a purpose."

American educator, stateswoman, philanthropist and founder of Bethune-Cookman College, Mary McCleod Bethune,[5] said, "If we accept and acquiesce in the face of discrimination, we accept the responsibility ourselves. We should, therefore, protest openly everything ... that smacks of discrimination or slander."

Richard Wright, author of the seminal African American novel, *Native Son*, wrote in his autobiography, *Black Boy*,[6] "Wherever I found religion in my life I found strife, the attempt of one individual or group to rule another in the name of God. The naked will to power seemed always to walk in the wake of a hymn." He went on to say, "I feel that for white America to understand the significance of the problem of the Negro will take a bigger and tougher America than any we have yet known. I feel that America's past is too shallow, her national character too superficially optimistic, her very morality too suffused with color hate for her to accomplish so vast and complex a task. Culturally the Negro represents a paradox: Though he is an organic part of the nation, he is excluded by the ride and direction of American culture. Frankly, it is felt to be right to exclude him, and it if felt to be wrong to admit him freely. Therefore if, within the confines of its present culture, the nation ever seeks to purge itself of its color hate, it will find itself at war with itself, convulsed by a spasm of emotional and moral confusion. If the nation ever finds itself examining its real relation to the Negro, it will find itself doing infinitely more than that; for the anti-Negro attitude of whites represents but a tiny part-though a symbolically significant one-of the moral attitude of the nation…Am I damning my native land? No, for I, too, share these faults of character! And I really do not think that America, adolescent and cocksure, a stranger to suffering and travail, an enemy of passion and sacrifice, is ready to probe into its most fundamental beliefs."

These are only a few of the African American thinkers, scholars, and leaders, who spoke or wrote in the early part of the 20th Century about the negative effects of slavery, racism, and Jim Crow on America and its people of color. However, unfortunately, these words ring as true today, in the beginning of the 21st Century, as they did then. Now, over a full century later, there are conversations and debates about whether there should be conversations or debates about racism in America. Obviously, racism and racial polarity are still challenges in the life of the American people and perhaps in the world as a whole.

When I was a young man assisting my grandfather in planting and harvesting the vegetables with which he used to provide for the family, I learned about the weed called, "nut grass". Nut grass is a wild grass that seemingly grew everywhere in our small, Northwest Florida town and it was the scourge of small farmers and homeowners who were trying to cultivate healthy crops or lawns, because it would take up the space for preferred grass and plants. This was because nut grass' top half could be cut to the ground level and yet miraculously it would grow back, almost immediately, as hardy as it was before. I quickly learned that to get rid of nut grass, permanently, you had to take the time to remove the nut grass plant, totally, including its roots.

Consequently, I have concluded that unless racism's roots are removed completely, like nut grass, it will continue to flourish and plague the lives and culture of the American people and perhaps the world at large, regardless of race, ethnicity, or communion. In consideration of this challenge I offer some musings on racism, religion and reconciliation of one of the premiere religious leaders of the Twentieth Century and early Twenty-first Century, Imam W. Deen Mohammed.

My sincere apologies are extended to those whose sensitivities may be hurt by what I have compiled in this publication. However, if we never have the courage to examine the roots and causes of racism and its possible resolution, we will never be able to eliminate it or its effects on us now and on our future generations.

Ronald B. Shaheed, Editor

Introduction

We call it our first experience with the Honorable Elijah Mohammed. His teaching was an experiment for us who were disconnected from our past history and introduced into the southern plantation slavery system; a system that was designed to test the human spirit and the human nature to see that if everything that supports that spirit and nature is taken away, to see that if that human spirit and human nature is deprived of that which supports it, could that human spirit and nature survive; and, is G_d's word really true? Is His plan and strategy practical? "We are going to test the blacks to see if they can survive with their human nature and spirit and to see if they can rise without getting help?" That was the plan for us and then the Temple of Islam came as a plan to prove that though we had been lost from self, lost from our purpose on this earth, we could be reconnected. So, Mr. W. D. Forty, I call him...You know him as Mr. Fard, Professor Fard,[7] he came and established the Temple as an experiment to see if we could rise; and he believed with all of his heart and being that we would rise, because he said it.

Start over again as a people

You are not people because of your physical contents. You are people because of your spiritual contents and your soul, psyche. When the ancestors of African American people were enslaved and cut off from past experience as a group, the past history, the past traditions of our group or members of our group; when we were cut off from that and had no way of continuing that life, that cultural life, that mental life, we had to start all over again, in a reality that was harsh, painful, and unwanted. We had to start all over again as a people. Now this was the case. This is true for the great majority of those that were put in that circumstance, made slaves in America.

Blacks died as people mentally

There were very few exceptions where a kind master had a slave and permitted that slave to keep his original mind, the mind that he brought, or that came with him from across the waters. That was very rare. In time, they died out and there are hardly any traces of their influence or their effect on the life of the rest of African Americans. So, as people we actually came to a death point, the point of death as a people. We died as a people and then we had to come to life all over again in very, very unfavorable circumstances. So, whatever choices we made, we made as subjects, not as free thinkers. We did not make choices as free thinkers. We made choices as subjects until we got some free thinkers like Frederick Douglas and we started to give birth to some free thinkers. G_d's Plan is just and poor situations sometimes produce the best human beings. Look at the beautiful poor people that came out of the poverty of knowledge, of the intellect and the land; poor land and poor intellect. But look at the wonderful people that G_d has produced.

Enslavement of black people

I have looked at the enslavement of black people and it used to set off in me ugly emotions, sometimes, when I reflected on what was done to our people. But G_d has blessed me to overcome that hurt. I have overcome that now and I know that no man can do me any wrong that G_d has not given permission for. And if I can see the wisdom of G_d and turn my hurt into a positive force that will make me more human and a better human person, oh, I will be so much enriched by that bad experience that G_d permitted for my future good.

Everything done for future good

Now, I believe everything is done for a future good. You know when you study psychology without Scripture you see G_d as a bad Entity. Yes, many psychologists, American psychologists, they have seen G_d in Religion as really the problem. That's because they do not know G_d's Word and G_d's Way. But we who G_d have blessed to embrace His Word and to appreciate His Will and His Way, the Ways of G_d, we are supposed to do the best we can with our life; do always the best we can with our life and to change circumstances for the better. But if we cannot, then know that it is in the Plan of G_d and G_d, if He wants to, will change the state for us. He will change the circumstances for us. He will change our state into a beautiful state. As He promises in Scripture, He will change your state into a beautiful state. That's what G_d will do.

Not enslaved by racism

Every hurt is not intended to be a hurt. A lot of hurt is intended to wake up our conscience and sometimes G_d sacrifices some of us to wake up the conscience of many. And even the individual will be rewarded immensely, if he will keep faith, remain faithful to G_d. This is my strong belief and I am a free man because of this belief. My belief has freed me. I am not enslaved by racism. I am not enslaved by any kind of arrogance or selfishness. I humble myself, make sajdah (prostration) in my soul to G_d, because I know it is only because of G_d that I have become this person that I am; and that is what I take great pride in. That is what I cherish more than anything else.

Freedom for the soul

It is not to have millions of people say that Imam W. Deen Mohammed is a good leader. It is not because of that. It is because I have found freedom for the first time in my life. It is not the freedom of my body, but it is the freedom of my soul.

My soul is free and at rest for the first time in my life. There is no freedom as sweet as the freedom of the soul, because G_d has created the soul to make us aware of the need to free more of ourselves. You could free your physical body and your soul is still there telling you, "I am not comfortable yet!"

There are beliefs in certain parts of the world that everything has a soul and that nothing is without a soul. When they say, animate, they are coming from that belief of those people. Animate means to give life to something that you regard as dead. You make it look like it is living and has life. It is called animation. Walt Disney is good at that. They lead the world in animation. I was born to teach. This is my life. I enjoy teaching. I knew I wasn't supposed to be a preacher because every time I would go home I would regret it. I would feel so bad when I would go home and sit down saying, "I just lost myself screaming like a nut."

Most Americans, their material possessions have become more precious than their own lives. They value them over human life. You can hear them say, "Get off of my new couch"; or, "I'll kill you, you little nappy-headed so and so!" They are speaking to their own children, now that material things have become dearer to them than human life and their own children's life. That is a shame. But that is the way the world today goes.

No persons anymore
They say eight people, now, not eight persons. Now, relatives are nothing but people, friends are nothing but people. You wonder how that happens. They put somebody in a scene. "They", meaning those who plan our life for us. They plan our spirituality for us, plan our emotional make up. They plan our feel for things. They plan all of that. They are in the waters of our life. Somebody is put among you to say, "Who are those

people. How many people are there?" The ones here they pick it up and pretty soon it is picked up. Then that justifies them. The same organized group that controls the media then put us on TV saying, "How many people do you have with you?" Once they do that, put it on television, or on the radio, on the records, then it spreads like wild fire all throughout the whole society.

They justify it because most of them do not know what they are doing in those roles. So, they justify it. If I were to get on a show and the host asks me, I would bring this point out and criticize this language to say how it is making us more impersonal and treating us as though we do not care about each other. We are not persons anymore. "Not persons anymore," means you have no human personality and that is the reality. So they are just telling you what they have done. You are no more persons. You are people. You have lost your personalities. You might say, "Everybody has personality." Yes, but some personalities are formed by media, entertainment, and by the culture; and when the culture supports you keeping a human personality most likely the public we look at will be in their human personality. But if the culture wants to change it, the change comes about by the hand of entertainment media.

Technology forming the spirituality of the masses

So, if they want to change us they can do it, if we are not grounded in the life that we choose for ourselves. We have to be in the life we choose for ourselves and that life has to be given to us from our sources. If we do not have a source for our life, for feeding our life and keeping our life in the picture we want it in, then we are exposed to all of these influences and our life goes from one thing to another.

Look at how they create us. Do you remember the black persons who used to be in the streets with us when we were

boys? They look similar to black people today, do they not?
These black persons, they have a new spirit, an image to be
associated more with technology than with human nature. What
I am looking at tells me that the world of technology is
contributing to the formation of the spirituality of the masses.
They are not just showing us robots. They are showing us
ourselves. They are making us robots.

Every animal of the forest

Isn't this a big game? And what does Allah say in the Qur'an?
This world is nothing but sport and play, or games and
amusement.[8] That is what this is in the Qur'an. G_d knew that
this thing was going to get bigger and bigger. It has gotten so
big, now, until you can hardly find persons. You only find
people. The Qur'an says there were those who were reduced to
monkeys and pigs. I think it was translated, apes and swine.[9]
The Arabic word, "Qirdatan", is the common monkey. Apes are
a little bit sober. Monkeys are silly. There is a difference
between apes and monkeys. An ape has a serious look on his
face. You do not play with him. But that monkey is full of
foolishness all the time, everything he has is for fun. His tail,
his head is for fun; his sex organs are for fun. That is to show
us G_d created everything to show us what is possible for
ourselves.

        A great philosopher once said, "In human life there is
every animal of the forest." That means of the world. And if
G_d has made us imitative, we are impressionable and
imitative. Whatever is outside we can take it inside. We breathe
out, we breathe in. Therefore, whatever is outside we can bring
it inside. When you do not use your valued life that Allah
created for you then you are vulnerable to be anything that gets
your notice. Now you have lost yourself. So now the monkey

comes into your life and you become the monkey, the pig, the ape, or the wolf, etc.

I know you have seen all of these animals and I mean at home, or at least on the block in your neighborhood somewhere. The elephant and every animal you can think of I have seen. We have it. The loud person that is the elephant. Sometimes, he wants to be announced. And the snake makes no sound. He is as quiet as he can be. I have had more snakes in my life than I asked for.

Hearts and sentiments have to be truthful
You can rehearse, or record in your mind, in your memory banks sciences and great knowledge. But if the attitude of your heart is immoral you will use that knowledge foolishly and that is the problem we have. On the one side, we have people who exercise their rational muscle for material ends, but do not exercise their moral muscle for human ends. We expect from those people great wisdom and great sense, because they have degrees from colleges and universities. However, that doesn't mean a thing if their hearts and sentiments are hypocritical. Your hearts and sentiments have to be truthful. The brain works best, in fact. It works logically only when the heart's sentiments are truthful and the brain is rational. That is why the heart is first. We are told in Al-Islam that Allah looks not to our faces but to our hearts; and we are told, also, that matters are judged by intentions.[10] We are told, also, that G_d changes not the state of a people until they change the attitude of their hearts. I can go on repeating this, that first you must have the right attitude of heart. You have to have upright sentiments; truthful, upright sentiments for your intelligence to work correctly.

Beauty not in color of skin
If my skin is black, I am not ashamed of my skin. I accept my skin and I think black skin is as beautiful as any other skin. I

have seen the blackest of skins and I have seen the whitest of skins and I think the beauty is not in the color, but in something else. So, our concern is to bring attention to our life, the identity of that life, the purpose of that life. I am a man. I am a human being. All of that is good. Our Religion tells us all of that. But what our Religion tells us, I would say with greater concern, is that we are a community. Our Religion wants us to see ourselves as a community, as community life. We are members in that community life. We must recognize community life, support community life and seek to improve or advance community life.

Community identity more important

G_d didn't say to us, "You are a black race". No! That is not in the Qur'an! G_d didn't say, "You are a white race! You are a black race!" G_d says, *"I do not look to your faces. I look to your hearts"*.[11] That is what G_d says in our Holy Book. He is not concerned with your black face, red face, yellow face, white face, or what color face you have. Nowhere in the Book does G_d tell us about our race! He is not concerned about our race. G_d says, "You are a community!" He says, *"This, your community is one community and I am your Lord; therefore, worship Me"*.[12] What He means by that is this. Your community identity is more important than personal identity, more important than racial identity and more important than national identity.

Do not look at faces, wealth, but the heart

G_d created these differences, too. But, He does not look to these differences. G_d says He does not look to our faces, but He looks to our hearts. You take a whole lot of human hearts and just lay them on a table and you couldn't pick my heart out. They would look so much alike that you could not identify the race a particular heart belongs to; because that is not an African heart. That is not a European heart. That is a human heart! So, when you look at the vital organs of human beings they all look alike. In the most important things in our physical make up, we all look alike and that is the way it is for the abstract body which is the more important body. It is my intelligence that is more important. It is my emotional make-up, my sensitivities, my human sensitivities that are more important. These are the more important things that identify me more correctly. It is not my skin color or the way may body is shaped. It is the invisible part that is the more important. And the truest part of me is my invisible self. That is the truest self.

Humanity is higher than race

 Muhammed, the Prophet, wanted unity but he did not want the unity that the others in his society wanted. They wanted the unity of Arabs. Muhammed wanted the unity of mankind, because that is what G_d made Adam for and created human beings to be; the unity of mankind; all human beings in one human family; to have that identity above all other identities. If human identity is put below any other identity, then we lose the quality of life.

       For example, this society treated us inhumanly when it made us their slaves over 350 years ago. They put our humanity under the nation and our humanity under their race. We say this because we are members of humanity. If their humanity has been put over the race it is a problem, because one's humanity is higher than one's race and it is higher than black. I can marry a black woman and I can have children that are Negroes. That is what they used to call us. I can have children that are black. But if I keep my human standard my children will not be lowered in quality, in excellence, or in their standing in society, if I keep my human standards.

But, are you human?

They missed all of that because they put so much emphasis on race saying, "I am a white man." But are you a human man? Frederick Douglas, the abolitionist, had to come back and show them that there is the self that G_d made; the human that is more important than yourself, the white, the red self, or the black, etc. So, he had to come and educate their people. A slave had to educate his former masters.

So, we did not have anything to happen in our life until Mr. W. D. Fard. We didn't have anything to happen in our life to make us reject the white world with all of its authority. Only Mr. Fard did that. He caused my father and many African American men and women to reject the white world and its authority, all of its authority, and follow him; follow him or follow his appointed leader, the Honorable Elijah Mohammed. And the Honorable Elijah Mohammed was such an obedient creation of Mr. Fard that he prepared us just as Mr. Fard intended. He prepared us to think independent of white authority. He put us in a position and a situation to be born as a people, again.

A new black being born

Some historians may not realize it, but it was not the Honorable Elijah Mohammed, but his son, Imam W. Deen Mohammed, Minister Wallace D. Mohammed, who sensed that a new people were being born on this planet earth. And thirty something years ago, maybe forty years ago, I told the followers of the Honorable Elijah Mohammed we are a new people on this planet earth. I said, "There never was a people like us before. We are the first and we are being created. Our creation is not finished, but almost." No, it is not finished, but almost finished. I do not know if you all can register the weight and significance of what I am telling you. But, to me it is actual fact, that I am a new creation on this planet earth and all those who identify in this thinking that was started by Mr. W. D. Fard are a new people on this planet earth, in actual fact.

All people once were savages

Naturally, African American genes go back to Africa, but that is not what makes us human, because Africans were once not human, just as Europeans were once not human. At some time in the history of all people they were not human. They were savages. They were just animals with human bodies, but were not human. I know some of you all, you are so sentimental you are saying, "Well, every child born of a mother, of a human mother, is a human". But, they weren't born of a human mother. They were born of savage mothers and they were savage babies. They came up as savages, not humans.

Human when Word of G_d enters person

You see the word, "Human", was not given to us from the secular world. The word, human, came to us from the spiritual world. And G_d said that He made man and when He breathed into him of His Own Spirit he became a living soul.[13] So really, if you are not a child of Scripture, a child of the Word of G_d, you are not human. I am not feeling for words and meanings here. I know what I am talking about.

     You are not human. In your vocabulary, yes, you are human, because in your vocabulary human means what the world has given you; the meaning the world has given you; the meaning you get in the schools and the meaning you get on the streets. Human means just a person looking like you, not looking like an ape or a dog, or something different. To you that is human. But that is not the original meaning of human. That is your meaning of human. The original meaning of human is a person that has become conscious because of the Word of G_d coming into that person. And the proof that it is only the Word of G_d that makes us human is that the populations of the world have only come into more human form as a result of the world responding more to the Word of G_d.

Not human before the Word

Even Islamic civilizations, when you look at their humanity, you may miss it. But, if you look at where the word started you will not miss it. If you look at where the word started with Muhammed, the Prophet, you won't miss it; and those that it touched from him, you won't miss it. But when you look at the Islamic populations, you will miss it.

Now, look at Christianity. Christianity started with Jesus Christ, peace be upon him, according to their understanding and from his disciples it came. Then, a new following came. Those who were in paganism before converted to Christianity and when they converted they did not show us humanity. In time, they showed us barbarity. This is a fact. The Christian world showed us barbarity, not humanity, why? It was because the word was not in them. The word was not in them and they were responding to an invitation to become the new rulers of the earth. I can keep on going showing you examples.

Human a term from Scripture

Look at the early followers of Mr. W. D. Fard. How sweet they were. How human they were. Then, look at the group that came in during the 60's, when the streets were all disturbed and violent and whites were mistreating us, cruelly mistreating us. A new breed came into the Nation of Islam. They came in because they wanted to be the new black man. They did not come in because they wanted to get closer to G_d. They came in because they wanted to be the new black man. So, that group, to me, looked like tin soldiers. They did not look human to me. They looked like mechanical people, although some of them were very human. But, their posture, their gestures, their mannerisms, their walk and their ways, to me said, "This is a mechanical person". Unless the Word of G_d comes into you, you are not human. Human is a term that comes from Scripture, not from the secular world.

No chance to be human

When science describes us, they do not describe us in that language. Humans, they say, are homo sapiens and they are themselves (scientists) also students and followers of Scriptural readings. So, they take the homo from human, or ground, the earth, and they have sapiens, meaning, thinking or having intelligence and they add that to it. Are they saying something different than what Scripture is saying? No, the only thing they are doing that is different is they are not giving credit to G_d for it. When G_d says, *"And when I have breathed into him of My Own spirit"*,[14] G_d is saying, "When I have made this vessel intelligent in accord with My Own Will, then he will be human and you have to recognize him." That is what G_d is saying.

In sociology, the field of sociology, you will learn if you have not already learned, that they have studied and done tests and they know that you can be born in human shape, a human body; but, if you do not have a chance to be put in a human environment, a social environment with human beings and have an opportunity to experience learning in a social environment with other human beings, you will never become human. So, human is not something that comes about because of you being biologically or physically made. It comes about only when a certain thinking comes into your head that lifts you above the animals.

An artificial people

We should understand that. So, blacks as a people we have been created since slavery. We are being created because we have been killed as a people. We were killed as a human group, although some humanity was left in us. As a group, we were killed and that humanity that was left in us could not reconstitute us or form us, again, a human group. It is just now happening. It is just now happening that we are really becoming a true human group.

There is a book that caused a lot of disturbance. It is called, *"To kill a mockingbird"*.[15] The white man in his cultural expressions (books, movies, music, etc.) has been telling us over and over again that we are an artificial people and that is what he means. He hates his own creation. The doings of his own world have given birth to an artificial people and any true person just cannot be comfortable with an artificial person.

Racism's position is artificial

So, a lot of this racism, hate, that we see, just real bitter racism that we see in this world today, it needs to be explained by those who have studied this thing as psychologists, or as students of psychology. And when we understand it, we come to understand that racism is a very, very complex thing. It is not easy to explain; very complex.

Language has served racism in the world, especially in America. And that is just where the biggest creation of racism is, right here in America. The language has served to make white people feel that they are different, special and superior. But it has also hurt them, because that position is artificial. That is not true. That is not reality. So, it has made white people artificial people. They have an artificial reality to deal with and then it made their subjects also artificial. Now, they have a second artificial reality to deal with. Their subjects, now, are trying to understand the people who made them their subjects and they are speaking from artificiality. They are thinking from artificiality and speaking from artificiality.

A battle he can never win

So, he (the black man) has a battle that he can never win. He will never win the battle until he discovers his own artificiality and discovers the white man's artificiality. And no one made it possible but W. D. Fard, for us. No one made it possible but Mr. W. D. Fard. W. D. Fard put us on an independent path to find truth for ourselves, rejecting all authority from without. So, Mr. Fard said to the world of white supremacy, "You made your man, but now I am making my man and I am showing you where you went wrong. "Now my man is not going to go wrong, because I have put him on the road to even think beyond me. I have freed him to think beyond me".

Now, that is a real teacher! That is a real parent and a real teacher! You see, a real parent doesn't want to hold the child forever. A real teacher does not want to hold the student forever. But he wants to prepare them to stand on their own legs and go even beyond what the teacher or the parent offers the child or the student. I thank Allah we are a new people and what does it prove? It proves the great worth of the human essence; that if the human essence can be put back in a normal, natural situation, the human essence will find itself and be formed the man, again. That is what it proves. I am the living proof of it.

1
The Origin of Racism

Many centuries ago, in ancient days, the Aryans from the North came down upon the dark people (Dravidians) around the hot belt in India. Failing to defeat them with physical force, they went back and studied the wisdom and knowledge of the people they failed to defeat.

A people's knowledge is their strength. You are no stronger than your knowledge. The world in ancient days was much like it is today. But, it was worse in the respect that only a few held the knowledge. Society was young and the knowledge was not trusted with the many. A few directed the people with as much knowledge as they thought the people could bear. The majority of the people were babies in knowledge. When the Aryans returned to the world of old with a new interpretation of the knowledge of the Dravidians, they began to feed it to the people of that ancient world.

Dravidians of the Indus valley

The Dravidians were ancient black people of the Indus valley of India.[16] Their name is from, "Dravida," which was the name of an old district in Southern India. The black people, i.e., the Dravidians, began to be frightened and thought that the Aryan (Caucasian) was a superior man that Almighty G_d had sent to punish them for their wrongs and that they were to take over the world. They believed this because in the Scripture of the Dravidians, the physical sun represented their body of Divine knowledge. Night represented ignorance, or the absence of that Divine knowledge. They did not arrive at this kind of language because of any interest in the night's blackness.

Children of the night

The Aryan people who came down from the North gave their own interpretations of Dravidian Scripture and spread it to the common people. The term, "Aryan", itself, reflects the deceitful scheme of those conquerors who applied this name to themselves. It is derived from the word, "Arya", meaning, "Lord" or "Master." The term Aryan has been used extensively in modern times by the Nazis in Germany (and even in America, today) who defined it as, "A Caucasian of non-Jewish descent." When Dravidian Scripture spoke of, "Children of the night," it was identifying a certain society of people who were weak-minded and weak, morally. They did not want truth because truth required them to grow morally.

They arrived at this kind of language because of their study of the nature of the sun and the nature of darkness. The sun is not only a source of light that enables us to have knowledge of what is around us when day comes. But it is also a source of energy and warmth. It comforts us and feeds us with energy. It makes weak physical life grow strong. The ancient Dravidians used the sun as a symbol, not of their god in body, but of their god in the body of that divine knowledge.

Children of the divine

No man can keep growing in real knowledge and remain small, morally. Any man that grows in real knowledge and remains small, morally, hasn't even known the knowledge that he has been following. He has been growing mechanically. The conquerors from the North said that the children of darkness were the black people (Dravidians) and the children of light were the Caucasians (Aryans).

Because the mass of the people were babies in knowledge and they saw that the Caucasians were advancing, they gave in to the Aryan reinterpretation of their Scripture.

They began to believe themselves that G_d had sent the Aryans (Caucasians) down from the North to punish them. They also began to believe that the Aryans were the children of the Divine and that they, the original inhabitants, were the children of darkness (ignorance which is not accepted by G_d). That made it possible for the Aryan people to trigger Aryan white supremacy in the minds of that ancient black people and they won control of the land of the Dravidians.

Modern day white supremacy

So, we understand the new, modern, white supremacy that has given birth to Ku Klux Klan[17] terrorism and all the other horrible teachings that we hear coming from deranged minds. This new world of white supremacy is really a rebirth of the old. Modern day white supremacists looking for something else to give them an additional weapon or power to conquer the world, came upon the old teachings of the ancient Aryan conquerors. They taught this, again, to the descendants of that ancient Caucasian people. They did an even more masterful job on the white supremacist mentality and made it even more powerful and more effective. They identified black people with lower creatures and spread their teachings among the ignorant of our people and whether we accepted it or not, it influenced our behavior.

But the new teachers of Aryan white supremacy did even more than that. They put a representative of the typical Caucasian stock (blond hair, blue eyes and pale skin) on the cross as a, "divine image", for black people in the Church to feast their eyes upon. The ancient masters in religion saw the efforts working in the society to try to graft a color consciousness of false color superiority. They identified it in their prophecies and they told of the evils that it would bring

about on earth. Right in the Bible they tell of the evil
consequences that would fall down upon the builders.

Racism is very old

I think Muhammed, the Prophet, saw that the last days would
be the days when the world would have to accept that they have
oppressed human souls with no justice. There was no
justification for it. And the prejudice was there at that time, over
fourteen centuries ago. The attitude of the white one was to
think he was better than the black one. Racism is very old. As I
said earlier, I think it started in Asia with the Dravidic
Scriptures of the Asian people and in their Scriptures, they
describe people as, "Children of the light" and "Children of the
dark". What they meant was they were innocent. They were
talking about the spirit of darkness and the spirit of light; or the
plan of G_d that He blessed some to see. They are in the light;
then, the plan of G_d that most of the people are ignorant of.
They are in the dark.

In the beginning, darkness

That is what the Dravidic Scriptures were all about and Genesis
is the same. In the beginning, there was darkness and G_d
brought light out of the darkness.[18] That is what they are talking
about. But a person who wants to make money thinks, "These
dumb suckers here, black fools, they are the children of
darkness. G_d meant for them to be put aside or used." They
get that attitude and they are already weak. They are deceived.
Money can make you deceitful. Consequently, they are already
situated to be deceivers. It just made it easier for them and they
brought in racism. I think nobody used it better than the ones
who divided the world. They divided the world to make the
world racist. I am talking about the ones who want power, the
ones who want dominance, and want to be the ruler of the
world. They think G_d favored them to be the rulers of the

world. They are the ones who gave everybody racism, fun for fun sake, indecency, sexual corruption and perversion, etc., to destroy them.

Three colors in mountain

In the Qur'an G_d says observe the colors in the top of the mountain with their colors, some pure white, some pure black, raven black, like a raven bird and some red [19]...I am sure that is a reference to the racist, to the people of the world at that time and now. There were black people, there were white people and there were red people; or I might say there were black people of Africa, red people of Asia and other places and now that the world has been discovered, all continents. There were yellow people but it does not give it that way. It says the white, the black and the red; those three colors. And the three sons of Noah we can easily see those as representing the colors of the world of mankind, black, white, brown or red. The mistake that was made by people long before the days of Muhammed, the Prophet, was to read the language of the Scripture without the knowledge of interpretation and thinking that the black child in the Bible is the black race and the white purity or innocence in the Bible is the white race; and that the red race is all the rest of the people, the brown, the yellow; all of the rest. That is a mistake.

I believe that these things are no more than conveniences for people who do not want to find G_d, who do not want to find the reality for human beings in their constitution as living creatures and in their possibilities for developing the world. But they want to put themselves in a situation to dominate the ones that they have stigmatized, or blamed as the inferior or bad guys. I am convinced of that. I am convinced that they believe in this great Aryan superiority, the pure white race that Hitler used. And I am sure it goes back to ancient times, when the whites from the North on the continent of Asia came into India; came down from the North into the South and drove out the darker people; drove them further south and became, eventually, the rulers, the ruling class of India. I am sure that that racism also has its roots, or its beginning in Scripture.[20]

No pure race anymore

Some time ago, the *Chicago Tribune* newspaper devoted its magazine section to new findings on explorations in Egypt and they claim they found a statue of what they call a god that is the biggest ever to be found in Egypt. They found it under water. The features of Cleopatra that they had in this magazine are obviously what is called Negroid; whereas, the popular picture of Cleopatra is a woman with keen, sharp features. This one did not present that. It is a round face with blunt features obviously, Negroid. It does not have to be one hundred percent African and we are not, either. We are mixed with other blood, too, but predominantly of African blood. So, we are called African American.

That is the way it is for most people of the world. They say there is no pure race anymore. This is what the scientists say. So, nobody has all of their blood. They are mixed with somebody else. And another thing of interest was that the find says that this was the Greeks' god. A researcher, J.A. Rogers, did a lot of study on this. He found that the Greeks worshiped black gods and it sounds ridiculous.[21] I was a young teenager about 15 or 16 years old when I read his books. That is when I got acquainted with him. He was popular, then, in the Nation of Islam. The ministers would talk to us about J. A. Rogers. He even visited the Temple of Islam and addressed us when the Honorable Elijah Mohammed invited him.

Greeks had gods that were African

Now, I am not taking that to be a joke anymore and it is not just because of what the magazine said. I read it in other publications by white authors after I got much older, who said that the Greeks had many of their gods as African. So, it seems that the Greeks had no problem with color. If they saw greatness in a people they wanted to include those people in their culture. Consequently, they included many African figures in their culture and among their gods.

Al-Islam opens your mind to many other branches of knowledge and it gives you a better understanding. If you study Arabic grammar your knowledge of English grammar improves. Just study another language and you understand English better. These languages help each other. It is the same thing with any field of knowledge that is universal. Islam is universal. So, if you study a universal knowledge it helps you understand something in that other area that you could not understand without the insight from your field of study; which for me is Al-Islam, the Qur'an, and Scripture.

Dr. J.A. Rogers

I am thinking and feel pretty sure of this. The white world, America, etc., is making those findings but this is no new discovery for the leaders of America. For the leaders of literature, etc., this is no new find for them. They knew about this. As I said, I read a white author who said the same thing Dr. J. A. Rogers [22] said, that the Greeks had black Africans as their gods. So, it is no new discovery for them. However, they have kept that back. Now, they say that they knew this and it had gotten to Southern businessmen and government people, the news of us being once in that kind of high position that even the Greeks had us as their gods. Most of the whites who came to the South were very poorly educated, and ignorant. They were just out of jail, a lot of them. They were told if they would come to America and work to help open up the new wilderness, they called it, the untamed, undiscovered areas, they would be released from jail.

Slave owners had no shame

So, they let out prisoners, all kinds of people and lot a of these people were very corrupt, very deranged, mental misfits. They let them come here because they needed labor. They needed anybody they could get and use, if they were not too crazy to dig a ditch. A lot of these people, because they were white, were able to make money and get blacks as slaves. A lot of these criminal types with messed up minds were able to get blacks as slaves and I believe the cruelty we suffered was mostly from these demented, messed up, sick-minded persons. I say that because some do not reflect on what demented means. By contrast, I was the type of student if the teacher said, demented, and I did not know what it meant, I would know what it meant if I heard it again; because I made a note of it and I looked it up in the dictionary.

They were very vulgar, nasty, very shameless people. They did not even have sexual decency. If they owned slaves it was nothing for them to do almost anything to them. They would beat them almost to death for little or nothing, torture, or do anything to them. They would use the black woman like they wanted to and had a white wife, too. They had no shame. Now, if that kind of people learned that the blacks they owned used to have whites calling them gods, can you imagine what was going to happen in their minds? It would cause them to detest and really hate blacks. There must be an explanation for that deep hatred because they are mostly out of it now. Most of the South, they have repented their hatred of us and they are nicer than most Northerners.

A white god for the slaves

That tells us they were not only ignorant, they were misguided, too, to believe that we were subhuman and beasts fit for what they were doing to us, what they brought us over here for; to be their slaves. I can hear them now whispering, the smart whites telling the ignorant whites, "You have these blacks who used to be called the gods." Then, what did they do? They put them over us (black people). They introduced a white god over us to pay us back, resenting, hating, what happened in the past. I believe this explains a lot of that.

Where is the white, blond-haired Jesus Christ that I saw when I was a youth? You can hardly find it anymore. That was the only Jesus Christ we saw in the African American neighborhoods when I was young. The picture of Jesus Christ was blue-eyed, blond-haired in newspapers or wherever you found it. On crosses in black people's homes, there would be a blue-eyed, blond-haired Jesus Christ.

Terrible things done because of fear

Why did he have to be blue-eyed and blond-haired for us? To make no mistake that the white man was black people's god. I do not believe the masses did this. I believe it came from the top, the smart ones. A lot of terrible things have happened and a lot of it out of fear; fearing that if we ever got independent, since we were that high over in Africa, we might outstrip them here and become the rulers of America. So, they had a lot of fear that forced them, drove them to do some of the things that they did.

There is a lot of evidence that the period of rule before what we know as the white man's rule was the black man's rule. Not only in that part of the world, but even in South America they found huge, big heads that looked like African heads and they don't know why they were there. They do not have any explanation for them. But when you look at them, they look like the heads of Nubians. They do say that the Fiji Islands were populated, originally, by blacks who found a way to cross the Atlantic Ocean in boats and come to that area; although a lot of them were brought there later to be slaves and indentured servants; a class a little above a slave, but not quite free.

"The browning of America"

I am inclined to really believe just like the whites ruled the whole world, now, it is changing. It is getting brown, as Mr. Johnson of *Ebony Magazine* said in an issue, *"The Browning of America",* it is now the browning of the world, not just America. It is changing and it looks like the brown peoples are going to be in power, not the blacks and not the whites. From the way things are happening, developing all over the world, it looks like pretty soon brown people are going to be in power. China has so many people and the Asians have so many people and they are intelligent. They are very smart and they are in such great numbers. Then, we have the mixing of races and browning has come by intermixing. So, it looks like a brown people may be in power soon.

Allah rotates the rule

Isn't that what Allah says in Qur'an? He says He rotates the rule to try people to see how they will behave or treat others.[23] And that is what we see when we study ancient history, medieval history and also modern history. When we study it, we see blacks, a long time ago, in power and I believe before that it was the people of Arabia. Mr. W. D. Fard, when he said the cradle of civilization was in Arabia, I think he had studied some of these reports in history. It seems that the Turks and Arabs of Arabia have ruins that go way back in the history of ancient times. Arabia has ancient ruins of an Arab civilization that existed and they had great buildings. They were great builders and they lost all of that.

Whites are predominant rulers now

The main thing I want you to know is that they are making new discoveries and it is changing opinions that they once had and there seems to be more and more evidence. In fact, the evidence, to me, is conclusive that at one time before the new West and before Islam, African people were ruling the whole world, like white people are doing now. White people are the predominant rulers now. They shape the world. Whether they are directly over countries or not, they are forcing countries to have to come to them or have to cater to them or bow to them. So just like that is happening now for the white people that used to happen for black people. Now, it is the white man's turn and the white man is losing his turn to the brown man. It looks like it is going to be soon the brown man's turn and after the brown man who knows?

I am a brown man. I did not get my color from the world. I got my color from science and science says I am brown and a black person is black. Science says there are no white people, except under their clothes. Whatever has been exposed is not white anymore. The sun changes its colors. Caucasians get red. They turn red in the sun and some of them are a little brown. But they are white folks by classification. Only a few of us are black by true description. Most of us are brown.

If you say wood is brown what about skin? An automobile, if you see the color and you ask what color it is and they say that it is brown, well, what about skin? You have a different rule for skin. The skin of the car has a different rule than the skin of the human being. This is a crazy world and these racist they are some crazy and insane people. They are manipulated by smart people who want to take advantage of all stupid people so they can rule the world.

Wise people not racist

The wise people are not racist. They know too much to be racist. They know that is stupid, but they are capitalists and greedy capitalists. They will divide people against each other; divide whole nations, whole races, whole masses of people against each other. So, the division that we have to become aware of that is really hurting all of us very seriously, the division we have to overcome if we expect for this world to really be humanized and we have governments that are humanized, civilized, is the division of the poor and the rich. We have to get rid of the poor, rich division where you have poor people being suspicious of rich people, not trusting them and thinking they are all crooked; and rich people fearing poor people, that poor people want to take what they have or rob and steal from them, etc. We have to heal that separation, that breach, that split that separates rich and poor.

Slave in some cases better than the master

The Qur'an heals it. In the Qur'an, you do not disrespect the person who has wealth. You respect them and you see their wealth as blessings of Allah to them.[24] A wealthy man is not to disrespect a man who does not have money or is a poor person. He is to respect that person as a human being and maybe that human being in his qualities is a superior to that rich man who has the money. He may be rich in material things, but that poor man may be his master. This is history, too. Many rich people have found a poor person, man or woman and the rich person saw in that poor person a wealth of knowledge, a wealth of character. So, they used that person to help them make their business and to make their profession successful. Here is a man with the wealth, but he is looking up to the poor man he has as his servant. He is looking up to him because he knows he has the knowledge that will help his business and he has the care and the character that he can trust. So, greatness cannot be measured by material things. That is why Muhammed, the Prophet, refused to ever have wealth.

2
Racism in Religion

Most of the culture of Western man comes from outside of the European people. The European people did not have much of a culture. Only very small parts of Europe had some culture and it is because the climate did not permit it. If you are facing cold weather all the time you do not have time to think about making all of these little nice drinks and a lot of fancy clothes. You want to stay warm. You want to get that meat, hunt it and get it quick, bring it in and eat it. You do not want to go outside and socialize. It is too cold. Europeans did not really come alive until others came in among them; then, they went out among others.

They were held back for a long time. So, when they came out they were angry and aggressive. But see how just G_d is? If He caused you to be denied, He made you to make up for it. He made your spirit and nature to make up for it. They have more than made up for it. Now, they are kind of getting bored and other people are going to take over. In fact, they are taking over. It is just a matter of time.

Everything comes out of the soul
According to what is happening right now in education, the Asians, the Africans, etc., are outscoring Europeans in colleges and universities. So, it is just a matter of time. Blacks ruled so long in Africa until we do not know when we are going to awaken them, again. It is in your soul. Everything goes back to the soul. Everything comes out of the soul and everything goes back to the soul. So, after your soul has enjoyed certain things so long you do not have any interest in them anymore. That is

not your interest. That is not your motive and that is not your spirit. You see the other people and they have the spirit to go.

Religion as psychology for dominating blacks

When the white man came out to see the world, who did he find in power? He found the black man in power. He had been in power for thousands of years, although the Asians had their time, too, and the black Asians were before the white Asians. This is documented scientific discoveries. The black Asians were ruling and they had great civilizations and then the whites came from the North and they discovered that something was happening down in the South. So, they went down into southern Asia and they found civilization there. They found a warm climate that permitted civilization to thrive. Then, they used religious psychology. Religion in the hands of the conqueror is psychology. They used religion as psychology for dominating blacks. They came in and found a people who were burned out on having a good time, so they were ready just to relax and they gave them the sedative of religion to have them cool out. They cooled out and the whites dominated them. Pretty soon the whites took over and ruled them until now. In Asia, the lighter skinned ones have been ruling, but now it is changing, slowly.

Religion made racist white supremacy possible

Do not just look at Africa and say, "They came in and they took over." It was not just Africa. That thing went all around the world. White supremacy went all around the world and it was made possible by religion. So, you tell people that dark is evil, dark is sin, demons are in the dark. You do not have to tell them that, "You are dark". They know they are dark and every time they look in the mirror they see a dark face. If they do not have a mirror the moonlit night and the water reflection will say, "You're black, man."

When you go to the preacher, he tells you all about the black demon. "That black demon! You had better be good because when you die the black demon will come at you, brother and you cannot escape the black demon! He will consume you, totally!" I am not talking about Muslims. This guy might be Hindu. He might be anything and he is preaching to the masses. He did not know that the ones held up in the mountains in the cold weather region were afraid and did not go anywhere. They found out something was happening down there in their land, so they gave them religion to take over their lives.

Religion altered to get people to accept dominance

That is why it says in the Qur'an, *"And fight them until religion is free for G_d."*[25] It means it has been used by man. He made religion to serve him and his desire for power and dominance. So, *"Fight them until religion is free for G_d".* This is in the Qur'an exactly the way I am giving it to you, *"And there is no more persecution".* [26]

It is not just talking about that immediate situation that Muhammed was experiencing. It is talking about religion, period! Religion in the world is mostly used to condition people to accept dominance saying, "You could have this whole world, just give me Jesus." And I have heard blacks say, "They can have the world, just give me Jesus." What do you mean they can have the world? They have had it for thousands of years before you came along and you sure did not give them permission to have it. There was a song, *"Sounds of the South"*, that said, "I have plenty of nothing and that's plenty enough for me."

Infiltrators among the poor to start new trend

The entertainment media initiates something in the public life, encourages something that is happening. But it is happening on a small scale, yet it is something they would like to happen on a major scale. So, they encourage it. Actually, they have infiltrators come among you and they act just like you and you think they are just like you. You think their interest is down there where yours is. They mix with you and start a habit and then they record the habit for the entertainment media, soap operas, or whatever and they put it out by way of the media.

It is fed to the public. The public grabs it right away and it becomes, almost overnight, the new life style of the people. It starts with language, or either a dance and language is always included. There is a dance and there is also a language to go with the dance. In the Bible it says, *"Let us go down and confound their language."*[27] It means confuse their language. Make it so confusing they will not be able to manage it. *"Let us go down and confound their language so that they babble and do not speak"*. This is in the Bible. It did not say let us devils go down. This is a people planning on how to conquer another people.

"A people no more"

Most of us have heard of the Tower of Babel, whether you go to church or not. It has been in literature, so you have likely heard of it. In another place in the Bible, it says, *"Let us cast their bands asunder so that they be a people no more".*[28] So, whoever was doing one thing, someone else is doing the other. The language is similar. It is obvious, no matter what the Bible says, who is saying these things. It is obvious that the same mind that said one thing is saying the other thing: *"Let us go down and confound their language so that they babble and do not speak"* and, *"Let us cast their bands asunder."* That means destroy their bands, throw them away, cast them off of them so that they be a people no more.

Who would want to target a people to have them not be a people except Satan, himself? The reality of that is before us as clear as it has been for any people who have ever lived on this planet. When you see that light-minded stuff, i.e., just having fun and seeking pleasures without fear of the consequences to family or whatever, that is what has destroyed family life for most people in America. It has cast the social bands asunder. That which holds husband and wife together, that which holds children and parents together, that which holds brothers and sisters together, that which holds neighbor and neighbor together, all of that is gone; not in the past, now. The public, most of the people of America today, have become a people no more. They are not a people anymore because their bands have been cast asunder.

Personality formed in group life
It is the same ones who have made the public, people, or the population no people anymore. It shows you that the mind of the Shaitan (Satan) is sick and he cannot be healed. They enjoy this game so much that they have to talk to each other. "Now, we have made them no people." If they are not people, they are not persons. Personality is formed in group life with other people. You have to be with people to acquire personality. If you do not have association with people, relationships with people, you do not have anything to develop your personality. Now they say they should not call each other persons because they are not persons. They should call each other, people. And they say, "How many people are with you?" They are bragging. That is exactly what they are doing.

Shaitan (Satan), Allah describes him (in Qur'an) when he is shown the man Allah wants to become the leader, or the ruler in the earth. He refuses to accept him by saying, in the Qur'an, *"Abaa was stakbara"*, translated, *"He refused and became exalted, bigoted".*[29]   The word, "Astakbara", comes from the root verb, "Kabara," or the noun, "Kabir", meaning, "Big". So, he became bigoted or he exaggerated his own importance. That is what it means. He became magnified in his own eyes and to himself he was much more important than the man G_d said He was creating.

"I repent nothing"

So, the influence that is Satan in the world, especially in the culture, comes from a person, or nafs (soul), described by G_d as one whose self-image is an exaggeration in his own mind. The word in the dictionary is, bigoted, or a bigot. That is what you called the racist with no education or a college degree who because you are black thinks he is better than you. It did not matter whether you were educated or not, he was better than you. That mentality is called a bigot, another term for the racist. Who is the biggest of the bigots? Shaitan, or Satan is the biggest. He exaggerated his own self-importance. He says (in Qur'an), *"You made me better than he. You made him of mud. You made me of fire that gives off no smoke."* It means, "I repent nothing". His statement means, "You made me and I repent nothing. Because I devote myself to intelligence, only, I have nothing to repent. I follow intelligence". [30]

It is reported that Prophet Muhammed said Jabril (Gabriel) was shown the world by G_d before the world was put into existence. He saw it as G_d made it before Satan influenced it and he said, "What a wonderful world! How could anyone go wrong in such a wonderful world?" Then Allah, G_d, showed it to Jibril after Satan had come and decorated it with temptations, allurements, something to attract you and take you off center, off of your natural course. Jabril said, "How can anyone go straight in such a world?" So, Satan made it very difficult for people to exist in that world influenced by Satan. It is very difficult for them to keep their moral life, their sensible life that G_d wants for them or that He made them for.

Satan is the game

Allah describes the world that Satan makes, also, as a world of falsities. It is a false world. It is not real. And He says of that world that it is games and amusements.[31] Therefore, many in the world are game players. Isn't that what they say in high circles? "They are actors". I know, because I have been among them. Often, I have been among them. They call each other actors and an actor plays a part. So, it is a play, an amusement. You can become occupied, glued to your own works, especially when your works are dominating how people live, how people feel and how people will treat each other. You can become so occupied with that and so glued to it that it is the most exciting thing in your life. It is just like a man who likes to play chess or whatever the game is. He can play it so much and become so great in it until he cannot do anything but live that game. I think that is what happens to Satan. Satan has played the game so long until the game has just taken over his ability to govern his own life. He cannot govern his own life anymore. The game is his life.

Satan not a person

So, he has to have fun, but he cannot come out and tell everybody what is happening. He cannot expose himself. So how does he relieve himself from that situation? He can't tell everybody what is happening. His pleasure is to watch his act and enjoy his act. He is getting great pleasure right now. I do not mean one being, but many living things. I cannot say, "Person". He is not a person. Many living things in human form are enjoying this. They talk to each other and they enjoy their act on the stage of the world, saying, "We are telling them now that we took them from being a people and they have no personalities of their own. All of them have the personalities that we gave them. Now we are going to tell them not to be persons, not to address each other as persons; but address each other as people, because they are people. They are not persons, anymore. They are the new people we have made. And we are going to give them their new persons. We made them people, again and we will make them persons, again."

This tells me that they are saying, "We are going to permit you to be persons, again. We have achieved what we wanted. We carried it as far as we can go that way. We have to bring you back home. We are going to let you be people, first, people we make and then we are going to send influences out to have you become human persons, again." What I know is that Satan is doing these things and if we really identify Satan, he is the game. And the players, they stay with the game because they keep each other in the know. Down through the ages they have trusted each other and no one can come in unless they identify them and know that they inherited this. It is inherited.

Choose life

We are looking everywhere and what you should see is right before your eyes all the time. The world has been made so thoroughly by this mentality that anywhere you turn for truth or evidence you are looking at their thing; that which is given to you by the same ones who masterminded this thing or just took over human life. It says, *"We give you two ways. Choose you life"*.[32] That is what it says. It did not say, "Choose you the way on the left", or, "Choose the way on the right". Why? It is because both of these are going to be deceitful. The left is going to be deceitful and the right is going to be deceitful. As a result, you children of this plan do not ever be with the lefties, those on the left and do not be with the ones on the right. You should stay with that which is in the center.

So here is the plan designed to rule the moral and rational life of the whole people on earth by a few. And the members in this original group they do not know what is going on, either. It is the masterminds that keep the secret with them. They do not want them to know this. Do not think a rabbi knows what I am talking about? He is just an innocent rabbi, most likely. What we see in the Bible that looks innocent, if you read it one way, it is beautiful and good. But they are not reading it the way we read it. That is their plan. They are reading the blueprint for the takeover of the world and the keeping of the world under their control.

Left means the unconscious life

We read of Moses in the battle against the enemy of the Jews and Moses has a man stand on his left and hold up his left arm. Another, stands on his right and holds up his right arm; and again, the word, "Arm". They are in battle and it says when they want to advance, the one on the right lifts his arm up to advance. When they do not want to advance the one on the left lifts the left arm up. This is confusing. Why would he not want to advance? Well, maybe they want to retreat. The left means the left life, the unconscious life. This is the army, right? This is no reflection on the United States of America or on our army. I do not believe they know what I am talking about, at least most of them do not. Maybe a very few in the top positions know what I am talking about.

Advance unconscious life, hold back rational life

When you start off saying, "Left, left, left", you are advancing by left. Why left and not right? Your right leg is your strongest leg. Why put your weakest leg before the right, the strongest one? You do not see the general in that group. So, they are saying these soldiers have been trained to carry out orders and not think. So, they have no head, they have nothing but feet. They are foot soldiers.

The unconscious life, it being the sign of Moses, means, "Advance the unconscious life and hold back the rational life and that will get them in position where you can bring back the conscious life and keep the world progressing for our purposes". That is exactly what is happening with the world. It says, *"As Moses was lifted up in the wilderness, so shall the son of man be lifted up".*[33] As Moses lifted up the serpent in the wilderness, so shall the son of man be lifted up. How was the serpent lifted up? He was lifted upon a cross, upon a check. The cross is a check, a stop. The son of man, is this the son of G_d? Why did they say, son of man, son of G_d? Who is this? At one time, he is the son of man and the other time he is the son of G_d. It did not say the son of G_d. It said the son of man.

Fight the schemes of Satan

Son of man means all human beings, all mankind. How do we lift them up? The same way Moses did, but not any real Moses. "Moses in our plan, our Moses. We will lift society up the same way according to our plan. We will advance their unconscious life when their conscious life gets in our way and when we get them totally under their unconscious life, then we will raise up their conscious life"; a master plan, the plan of Satan. Allah says, *"Fight the schemes of Satan".*[34] He did not say fight Satan. Where are you going to find Satan? How can you identify these people? He may look like he is Chinese. Some of them may be Chinese. You do not know who they look like. Some might be African. Who knows? I have seen some Africans looking like aliens, like there was nothing alive in the body, like a dead thing was there. Who knows? Maybe they have some Africans in that group, too. We do not know.

It was initiated by those people who think their race is the chosen race and everybody else is supposed to pay homage to them. Are they the designers? No, they do not know what is going on. This thing is too subtle for us to identify them. They would not be identifiable. They would not be under any name and it is because they are too smart for that. The Qur'an says, *"They write Scripture with their own hands and say this is from G_d"*.[35] Allah has told us all of these things. Where are the Scriptures the Qur'an is talking about? They have to be somewhere. If we believe in the Qur'an we know those Scriptures are somewhere. You cannot put your finger on Satan. You cannot identify any living form that is responsible for this. They are too smart for that. But we should fight the schemes of Satan and not just the vices that are in the world.

His biggest scheme is manipulating human life, changing human morality whenever he pleases, or managing the world as he wants it managed. And how does he want it managed? He wants it managed for money. This is in the Qur'an and Bible, too. It says his greed is for material power, because he knows if he gets the material power, then he has that which every life is supported by; and you will have to have great moral strength to say, "No", to him when he says, "Your only opportunity to progress materially is to accept my world and not make any trouble for me".

G_d takes over your protection
It takes great moral strength to say, "No", to him when you know that he can shut you out of everything, all material opportunities. But he cannot do any harm except as G_d permits. When you give yourself totally to G_d, then G_d takes over your protection. You do not have to worry about it. I fear nothing. Nobody can harm me, no government, etc. They have no power to touch me, believe me. They hear these things but

they do not have any power to hurt me or to touch me. Allah would not give me this understanding to hurt me. If it were going to hurt me He would not let me get it.

I do not worry about them at all and I am not out to get them. I am after getting our people and good people in a situation like I am in so they cannot be hurt and cannot be mastered minded by wicked powers. That is all I am interested in and that is human. Human is wanting to support human beings and human life and wanting to help human life avoid trouble, problems and death. The worst death is moral death, not physical death. That is nothing. Physical death leaves no pain. Moral death pains all the time.

Patterned on principles of the universe

Man comes up believing that his own structure holds up the world, so he has to die to himself. He has to die to himself and come out of the ideology that says man is the center of the universe and accept the higher concept, that man is a form patterned on the principles of the universe. Allah says, *"Think not, oh man, that your creation is a bigger creation that the heavens and the earth"*.[36] That is to tell us, "Do not believe in the old Jain idea". Some of you perhaps studied the Jains and Jainism. They were an old, ancient people, long before Christianity, who believed that man was the center of creation and that his form was really the whole for of the universe. They believed that if you could take a picture of the external world, you would see the external world existing in the form of a man. And didn't the Greeks and some other mythologies present the universe like that; that actually man is the microcosm and the external world is the macrocosm? They presented the idea that really there is a big man out there giving birth to little men and the concept of G_d is man; and G_d made man in His own image and likeness. This comes from that faulty concept of theirs that the external world is a man, too, and it is G_d. The entire creation, the entire reality taken all together is the G_d and it gives birth to man in its image; the microcosm. This was their idea and this is still the idea in many of those myths and religions today.

Material world holding man up

But, this is not Al-Islam. The idea in Al-Islam is that man is a unique creature in the creation and that he has evolved or been formed just like all other creatures in the creation; and the external world is not the type bigger than the original type. It is not that he is a microcosm or a small miniature picture of that. No, it is that there is a material reality out there and he is one of the principles of that material reality. The laws that govern his particular form are established in that outside, external, material reality. That is what it establishes; not that the external, material reality should conform to his reality. This is what those myths say, what Jainism says. If you want to know what should be the rule in the outer world, study man and apply the knowledge that you find in man, in a study of man to the other world; whereas, we are taught, no, study the outer world; then, apply the knowledge that you find in the outer world to man, because it is man's bones holding man up. It is the material world holding man up; for his material structure is nothing but bones of the material world; nothing but material matter that has formed of the material world and has taken that shape. It is the material world that has evolved his skeleton. Do not just look at what I am saying. Look at what this points to.

Above you are seven

Now, we see that in the Qur'an, basharan or bashar, are connected with teen. He created basharam min teen.[37] This higher sensitivity, it is created out of this willing obedience in man; willing obedience, or the natural, inherent nature to obey in man. Then he becomes conscious and of that same nature is created a higher skin, a higher sensitivity, an outer skin. And so he becomes bashar, or khalqan akhar.[38] Then G_d says, *"And above you there are seven strong firmaments and in you, a like number"*. [39] So now we have a higher number than even the ones that we have been discussing up to this point. How are we to understand those strong firmaments in the ascension and travel of Prophet Muhammed, peace and blessing be on him? In the Ascension (Mi'raj),[40] he saw men in those graduations. Adam was on the first level. Jesus and his counterpart, John, were on level two. In other words, we have two on one level. On the third level, he met Joseph and on the next level, Idris. On the fifth level was Aaron. He greeted Moses on the sixth level and Abraham on the seventh. These represent what? The seven strong firmaments. So, there is a sensitivity in man. Then, there is a conviction that G_d wants. G_d wants that sensitivity to conform to a logic, to a truth, where that sensitivity becomes a conviction. Adam was a man of conviction and every other man that goes up that line to Abraham, including Abraham, men of conviction; strong firmaments, men of conviction.

What made possible their convictions? The same nature. Upon seven He built seven. Upon seven, the nature, He built seven. But how do they come into the higher conviction? G_d reveled to them the knowledge of the external world. He connected their reality with the external reality. He showed them the basis of their nature and their sensitivity in the external world. Therefore, their convictions became solid, strong convictions; convictions so strong that we see those convictions outside of us. *"And above you are seven, firm heavens"*.[41] And what are the heavens depicting? The universe. They are depicting the universe. So, man now has gone outside of himself and established himself in the universal order, in the context of universal truth. That is what established them on firm planes, very firm planes. But, they are no more than expressions that G_d created in him fulfilling themselves. So, it is the inner potential finding its place in the external world. We are simply talking about the connection between man and man.

Anthropomorphism

And what is our purpose in this discussion? Our purpose is to prove that idea of G_d manifest to be wrong, the idea of man-god. That idea of man-god came into Christianity from the Greeks and others that believed that. That is not Jesus' teaching. Jesus never taught anything like that. So, we should understand that this idea is foreign to true religion. None of the Prophets had that. It is foreign to true religion. Those people that had a different spiritual discipline, a different intellectual discipline, they are the ones who came to that kind of understanding. The idea of man as G_d was never a part of established religion. Anthropomorphism is what I think they call it. It means man-god, or god-man. So now we can see where this foolishness comes from. It comes from superstitions where man thought that he was the center of the universe and that his form was really a small copy or a small manifestation of the external world; that actually the external world was actually G_d and all-inclusive and it took the form of a man. If you look in the Old Testament this idea is there in very clear language. It speaks of lower regions as G_d's feet, higher regions as His bowels, where there is thunder and lightning. This is the Old Testament.

Pantheism

So, you can follow that kind of logic on to its conclusion; that is, that His head is above the clouds. His head is where the stars are. Now, if you look at the picture that they give you of G_d in the New Testament it shows this completed. It shows Jesus as G_d and it shows him with the sun as his robe. It shows sunlight as his robe and we know that sunlight is higher than the clouds. But it includes the clouds all the way down to the earth, the feet. It includes the clouds all the way down to the earth. Above the robe is what? The head. Above the sunlight, then, is what? The stars, the stars of the higher heavens. So, the New Testament gives us this picture of Jesus with the sun as a robe and a crown of stars on his head, meaning that he is, The G_d, the macrocosm. Jesus Christ is the macrocosm and G_d is no more than the external reality. This is pantheism.[42] It is akin to pantheism and if you do not think this is what those people believe in higher Christianity, in higher circles of Christianity, then take it from me. This is what they believe. They do not believe in G_d like the common people believe in G_d. They believe that the whole universe, the cosmic reality, is the only force we have to contend with. And they believe that man is an expression of what is in the total body of that reality. He is the manifestation of the potential or the inherent value in that whole body; that the big god gives birth to his son.

See Jesus as a black man

That is why they are saying now, "Oh, if you do not like Jesus in the form that he is in, well, it is okay. Every man should see Jesus in himself". Isn't that what they are saying? "If you are black, then, see Jesus as a black man. That is okay." That is what they say. Why? It is because they know in their logic man is the microcosm in the image of the macrocosm and Jesus so happens to be that. Now if you want to see that in your own form that is okay. They say, "Oh, we do not care. As long as you keep our brand of religion we do not care. It is okay. You can see it that way if you want to. You are still going along with our idea."

But, when you accept the Qur'anic idea, follow Imam W. Deen Mohammed and tell them, "No, we are not to see G_d in any form", that is where they break with us. We have differences now. But thanks be to Allah, the mind of humanity is growing. Each age brings about new developments. So, we found a lot of support from among even Christians for the movement to remove all images that attempt to portray the Divine. Praise be to Allah. And I hope this is an indication that there is a lot of support. But you do not find this support coming from the real top people. No, indeed! Why? It is because they are the ones that know what we are talking about now and they see that to accept what we are saying would be a conflict, would be in conflict with what they believe. However, many Christians who have not been allowed to come into these seminaries, because they have not been allowed into them, they are exposed to human influence; and when they see our logic they say, "That's humane. That is sensible. I support that". Whether it is a Catholic, Protestant, etc., does not matter. They support it. Praise be to Allah.

From one soul type

Do you think a Chinese baby cries in Chinese and laughs in Chinese? All of them were born to make the same sounds and having the same sounds, the same emotional nature, crying, laughing and smiling. The same soul, that is what it means. That is what that evidence says, that we have one soul. We come from one soul type, though we come into a world where we become different nations and different races. The G_d that made us made us one family, with one soul type.

In the Qur'an, G_d says He is the One Who gave us laughter and tears.[43] It means that the nature in you was given to you by your Creator. When we are born, all of us have the same language, then we learn different languages. Our language is the language of our soul. It says: "I hurt. I feel good. I am scared", etc. We used to think the white man could not be frightened. He kept us in so much fear. We thought he could not be made afraid; or we thought he was too dangerous to try to make him afraid. But all of that has changed now, because our people challenged him and saw that he could be made afraid. Frederick Douglass challenged his slave master. He got a second slave master who was mean, a typical slave master. One day, the history says, Frederick Douglass hit him. Frederick Douglass was a big, tall man. He hit him and knocked him down in the road and he got away. He went up North, finally, to Boston, Massachusetts. [44]

There is an explanation as to why they said that we were born with a curse on us and our color is a crime or a curse on us. I feel very sad to say to you that it comes from the Church, this idea. Muslims do not accept it, because we read the Qur'an and most Christian denominations do not accept it; that is; most churches do not accept it. But a few churches did and it might be a few churches that still do accept this Bible-based idea against us. But as you read on you are going to see that I have different thoughts even about that

The three nafs

We are taught in Al-Islam of the three nafs. Nafs means, soul or person. Most of the time, in Scripture nafs means the soul or the soul of a certain type of people, or a certain group. It can be even a certain nation that is in this behavior. They are characteristic of one of these (three) souls. Scripture gives these three, meaning that all people are characteristic of all of these three, some of these three, or at least one of these three.

They are called nafs, soul or persons. We were taught that these three souls, or nafs, are native, intrinsic to human life, to the life of all people; not just one people. This is Al-Islam. There were three sons in the story that I just mentioned to you or alluded to when I said it is in the Bible. There were three sons in that story, one was high-nosed, proud of himself thinking he is the best and highly critical. In the Qur'an for those who know the Arabic, it is, *"Nafsin lawwamah,"* the soul that is highly critical or very severely critical.[45]

Another of these sons was of the sentimental type. In the Qur'an, this is, *"Nafsin mutma'innah"*.[46] I do not know where they get this from in the Bible because I read the Bible. I have not read where Jesus cried in the Bible. But I know there is an expression of the church people. They say, "Jesus wept. Peter slept by the doorstep." Muhammed wept, too, and cried over the condition of people in the world; so this type. And I am sure Ibrahim also cried, because this was his type, "Nafsin Mutma'innah," the sentimental type. It is translated as one who is at peace in his soul, at peace in himself and at peace with G_d. People who are at peace with G_d, especially religious people who are at peace with G_d and are at peace with their own soul, they are people who are touched by the suffering and troubles of the world; and they, too, can cry.

Egypt was the leader of Africa

Lastly, there is the one, or the type that is called, *"Nafsin La Ammarah"*,[47] in Qur'an, our Holy Book and I am making the connection for these types in the Qur'an and Bible. You do not have to buy this. Students of the Qur'an do not have to buy this.

This nafs is the one (Ham) in the Bible that is called, "The one who laughed." The story goes like this: Ham was the father of three sons and the Bible said that Ham is Egypt and if you do not know it, Egypt is Africa. At that time, Egypt was the leading nation of Africa and Egypt has led Africa many, many hundreds and some say several thousands of years. It was first Lower Egypt in the beginning and it is where Sudan, the land of the blacks, is. The whites from the Mediterranean area they came easily to North Africa, because it is so close to them. But they hardly ever went down into the interior of Africa. They would do business with them but hardly ever would they move down there or establish themselves. They never did.

The first builder of the pyramids

South Africa is something new, white people living down there. The original pyramids, the builders that we know to be in Ancient Egypt were the blacks from Lower Egypt. This can be proven. If you just go to Egypt to see the monuments they will take you on a tour and you will see the evidence yourself. I have been there and I have seen the evidence. But my teacher that my father got to teach the high school students Arabic so we could learn later how to read the Qur'an ourselves in Arabic, Dr. Jamil Diabb, he told us, "The first builder of the pyramids, his name was, Meenah. He is the father of the pyramid building in Africa". This was a Palestinian telling us this. It was not one of us. Dr. Jamil Diabb said that later in the history of pyramid building, the North (Northern Africans) took it over and they became the pyramid builders. Now there is a great science in the building of the pyramids. It has a message for life, how life is constituted by nature and how you are supposed to preserve and build up that life. This is the mystical religion of the ancient people who built the pyramids.

The height of man's mind

This story of Ham in the Bible identifies Egypt as Ham. You can buy it or you do not have to buy it. Egypt in the Bible represents a highly civilized nation. So, they took a nation that represented a great and ancient civilization and they used that nation as a language; not to point us back to that Egypt, but to put in our mind a highly developed society in the sciences and in the spirit, etc. So, Egypt represents the height of man's mind and intellect. But Egypt had started to decline. They weren't building great pyramids and they weren't practicing these great sciences at that time. So, the ancient civilization of Egypt is personified; that is, you use a person to represent a highly civilized nation. Here, they represent that great civilization as a person and the person's name is Ham. The people from him are called the Hamitic race or people.

He lost his culture

It is said that Noah got drunk and was lying in the bed with no clothes on. This does not mean that he actually got drunk with liquor. But it means his mind became befogged with amusement and things. His mind was not what it used to be. His mind was not skillful and insightful as it was when they were building the great nation. He had become drunk in his mind, meaning that Noah had lost his balance and his soberness that he used to have for his intellect. He was naked, meaning his culture had gone and he was bare, naked, without culture. One of his three sons came to Noah and saw him in this state and he laughed. They said that son was Canaan and they said people of African descent are the children of Canaan. We are Canaan and we are the children of Ham, but through Canaan. So, the curse, according to the Bible, did not hit Noah, directly, for being in that condition. It hit his son. It fell upon his son, Canaan, and that is black people.

The Bible says that G_d decreed that Canaan, the sons of Ham, be reduced to servants and be made the hewers of wood, cutting wood and the totters of water, carrying water for the other sons.[48] Do you see how the picture is coming to light now? Do you see how the wrong-minded people could read that and say, "These black people are cursed and G_d decreed that they be our servants; to cut wood for us, do these menial jobs, these cheap, unskilled jobs and bring us water and tote water for us."

Secretly recognizing your value

Let me tell you what no one else is going to tell you. When they say, "Tote water," they are not really talking about toting water. When they say, "Cut wood," they are not really talking about cutting wood; although, that is what they are going to tell you, what it is, physically. But, when they say, "Cut wood", they mean that you are the one who is going to be skilled in the work of spreading love (wood). Wood is what makes people warm. When they put up a wooden house that is where they warm themselves. So, they think of wood as giving them warmth and wood is what they have the fireplace lit with. It warms the house. Therefore, warmth is associated with love. So, they relegated us to being hewers of wood and carriers of water.

Water means the spirit. You will carry the spirit. These were no fools who were assigning the jobs to the races of the earth. By my interpretation or translation of what I have read, if I am correct, you can see that these people were no fools. It takes great minds to come up with such ideas; to identify a whole people that they are putting down. But while putting you down before the eyes of their race, the white world and all people, they are also secretly recognizing your value. And secretly, they are going to rob you, like they robbed Christ before they crucified him, according to the Gospel. They are going to rob you of all your natural properties and all of your natural pearls and jewels and they are going to use them for their world at your expense. You are going into slavery. You are going to hew wood and tote water. But they secretly have another role for you in order to open up the wilderness for them.

Race problems from misreading of Noah's story

A great writer and a brilliant mind, James Baldwin, in one of his books that he wrote said the white world of white supremacy used us as a scapegoat. What I alluded to when I mentioned

Christ and African Americans is a people being used as a scapegoat. To take the attention off the suffering of all other people, they will make African American's suffering so severe that others will forget their suffering.

My studies of the story of Noah and his sons in the Bible and what I have found in the Qur'an that addresses the same story, would have me believe that race relations in America suffers because of a misconstruing or misreading of the Holy Bible's story of Noah and his three sons. It only says that Ham laughed. If Ham laughed and he was cursed, then his problem was that he laughed; and he laughed in a situation where he should not have laughed. His father was tipsy or drunk and in the nude, so he laughed. The next son saw his father and it hurt him. It was so shameful that he turned his head away and refused to look on him.

That is the, "Nafsin lawwamah." Nafsin Lawwamah will say, "Oh, this is despicable. This is shameful. I do not want to look at him." That kind of nature in us is highly critical, and that is why it is called Nafsin lawwamah. We will see faults in people and do not look for reasons; we see defects in people and do not look for explanations. We just say, "Oh! That is shameful"; and we become highly critical. These natures are in all people; these types or features of human nature.

Peace with G_d

The third son saw his father and he went and got some cover and put it over his father to cover his nakedness, so the Bible says. This is the, "Nafsin mutma'innah," the one who is at peace with his own soul and is at peace with G_d. This is called the tranquil soul, not troubled by what happens in the world. He is beautiful and peaceful. Abraham had such a soul. How do we know this? The Bible and Qur'an says that he was put into the furnace by his enemies. And whenever they would open the door to see how he was doing, they found him unchanged by the flames. Allah says in Qur'an, *"Flames, be cool for Abraham."* [49]

So, he was not hurt by the flames. This means that his soul was so much at peace with G_d and at peace with himself, that you could not take him out of his original nature. No matter how much suffering or pain (flames) you put on him, it would not change him a bit, i.e., the flames of corruption, the flames of hatred, the flames of anger, the flames of deceit, the flames of sin, the passions of sin. I speak to you from Scripture. I do not speak from my own mind. Some already believe that. One of these days more of you are going to know that I do not speak from my own mind. I speak from Scripture.

People of Moses Argued

The people of Moses argued with him all the time; they would not let him have any peace. They were slaves in Egypt, second class citizens or worse in Egypt and G_d blessed Moses with the guidance to lead them out of Egypt towards a land that would be their own. But they were a people who questioned him, did not have faith in him, just worried him and gave him all kinds of complaints all of the time.

G_d cursed them, as the Bible says, with fiery, flaming tongues. The tongue, your speech, can also be flames that burn like fire. So, Abraham being put in the fire, we do not know how many of these different types of fires his enemies put on him when they confined him to the fires. But whatever they did, Allah makes us know in the Qur'an that the harm could not reach Abraham, because he was Nafsin mutma'inah, a tranquil soul, at peace with himself and at peace with his Maker.

Blacks' emotionalism channeled to church spirituals

They say we are the sons of Ham. I know exactly what they are saying. Our humor is a birth defect in us. That is what they are saying; that, "These Blacks they are too full of fun. They laugh too much." So, I repeat now. Go back to what I was saying. If our humor is a birth defect preventing us from developing into mature adults, that extreme condition was channeled into Negro Church Spirituals, especially, since we have been on this continent. That extreme was channeled into Negro church spirituals.

Forming of the black church

If nothing else was done, the plantation life in America was enough to kill the tendency to laugh in us. That was no laughing matter and it lasted for a few centuries. It made us take up the church gospels. You have to remember that when blacks began as Christians in this part of the world, whites segregated them even in the church. They would not let them be in their section. They had to be in a section all by ourselves. This was such an insult and pain for black people in the church, that one of the leading Christian thinkers (Richard Allen) left the whites and formed the first black church, the AME Church, the African Methodist Episcopal Church.[50] It was African to connect with our own people, Methodist to connect with that branch of Christianity, and Episcopalian to also connect with the Episcopalians. But these terms that they have for different denominations in Christianity, they are given in the Bible, i.e., Methodist and Episcopalian.

So, I do believe that this new thinker leading black people from the white people into their own church, went to the Bible for those terms that he chose, himself, to develop his own African Methodist Episcopalian Church. I know they were deep, curious thinkers in the Gospel, because I've met some of them myself, since I have become a well-known person among religious leaders and I find them still to be very intellectually curious and studiously studying the Gospel. That is their tradition. They left the church of white leadership and they formed their own church. They were trying to save themselves from people who did not really like them or respect them as equal human beings in their creation or essence.

The Pleasure Principle

Taking up the religion of Christianity and becoming Christian in the Church and giving ourselves to the Gospels and to expressing our need for pleasure and joy through this medium or means, i.e., the Gospel in beautiful songs, that alone was enough to take African American life up from being just silly and fickle, to being serious and sober; thus, helping us to mature into rational adults. However, black people's nature for humor or joy, set them in a new behavior mold, if they were not already in that mold. I think it set African Americans in that mold because the slaves did not have anything to really shout about, nothing to really cheer them up. Slavery was too horrible on the plantation. There was nothing to cheer them up, except their reflection on a just G_d, a Creator, Who loved them. They did not have much to make them feel good. But then they began to learn the Gospel, the New Testament and began to see the beauty there and identify with Christ Jesus. The world had made them scapegoats. It pulled them close to Jesus, because they were seeing themselves in Jesus. They were seeing what the world had done to themselves through what the world had done to Jesus, according to the Gospel of the Bible, or the New Testament of the Bible.

Blacks' energy expression bottled up by slavery

This experience with the Church and the Gospel and singing made it possible for them to have their need for a pleasure expression fulfilled. In psychology, they call it the need for the pleasure principle. To have expression for that was now given to them, fully. You cannot take your body where you want it to go. You cannot do with your body what you want it to do because of discrimination, oppression and laws that were keeping you from doing with your body what others were doing.

Here was a lot of energy that could not be expressed, therefore, it found expression in any outlet it had. So, all of the energy that G_d created for us to plow the earth and to have farms to support our life, to have agriculture, to have industry, all the energy that G_d gave us for that that couldn't express itself in a world of white supremacy was all bottled up and had to express itself in any outlet available. The outlet that was available was the spiritual outlet and the beautiful language of the Gospel gave us food for our pleasure principle or our inborn pleasure needs that G_d created us with.

G_d planned for those who tamper with human nature
Look at how powerful black people became. But also look at how powerful those psychologists were who designed this plan; that black people be denied those things so that they would have to give all their energies, all of their capacity to express themselves, to the spirit. They were making black people a powerful spiritual force in America to use them to solve their problem. What was their problem? Their problem was our problem with them. Do you think they loved each other? They wanted to build a great world and were headed for a great destiny and they knew that they didn't even love each other. They had already been fighting each other in Ireland and Scotland and in different countries in Europe. They had been fighting each other in the Middle East. They had been fighting each other in Asia. They even fought each other in Africa. They are fighting each other all the time.

They were working for a world of peace, but they were planning the creation of a scapegoat. I will hold my tongue here, because it will hurt some Christians and it is likely that they will not understand it. But they made us a scapegoat. They planned its creation and then did it. They created their scapegoat. Do you think Allah, Who revealed the Qur'an to Muhammed didn't know this was going to happen? He says, *"Let there be no altering on the fair nature made by G_d."* [51] G_d would not say that if it were not possible for man to alter his own nature. G_d knows that man has the intelligence, especially using the tools that G_d provides him with, to actually study our constitution as a spiritual being, rob that, exploit it and alter it to his own advantage.

G_d says: *"Make no alterations on the fair nature made by G_d."* [52] But they did it and they paid a price for it and are still paying a price for it. But G_d has a way of taking the victim with all of his scars, wounds and pain and turning it around and making it work in his favor and for his better future down the road. So, they had the intelligence to plan, to dam up our forces, like a water dam and to channel them where they wanted our energies to go. They had the intelligence to do that. But Allah says, *"They plan and Allah plans and G_d is the best of planners"*.[53] So, He has already planned for such tampering and for persons with the mind to tamper with the nature He made human beings in. He planned in advance for them when He created us. He planned the defeat of those who would tamper with our nature, alter our nature and use our nature against us for their own benefit.

The rejected stone becomes the corner
The Bible says, the Qur'an says, and Muhammed, the Prophet, taught that those who are crushed down shall rise up to the top. The bottom rail shall become the top rail. *"The rejected stone shall become the corner stone"*,[54] meaning the main stone in the building. The mason, the first thing he wants is a right angle

when he is building. Then, the stone in that corner is the right stone that decides how the rest of the building will be lined up. *"And the rejected stone shall become the corner".* G_d is telling us how He is going to work against those who plan to use His people.

And do not think they do not use His people. G_d, in the Bible also says, *"Will a man rob G_d? Yet you have robbed me this whole nation."*[55] G_d is speaking of this whole people. Now who is this talking about? It is talking about the Jews, their Prophets, referring to the world that was dominating the lives of the Jews, like ancient Egypt. G_d was charging them with robbing Him, taking away from Him, their Lord/Creator, a whole people. Now what people were any more thoroughly robbed and any more completely taken from their natural relationship with G_d, the Creator, than the slaves of the plantations? None!

Create a new language to bring them back

So, you have to take them out of the language environment that they have been shaped and formed in, from out of their original nature and create a new language environment for them that will bring them back to have faith like a baby. So even after the Honorable Elijah Mohammed's teachings we needed another transformation. How are we going to get that transformation if we are not taken or weaned off of one language dependency and put on another language dependency? That is what had to be done and it worked. Once we are put into a world of a new language environment and we have faith in it, that language environment, if its direction is arrival at the Qur'an and Muhammed's leadership, once you get there, you are truly free. You have dropped all the wrappings of the old reality so that you come bare and alone, like a baby straight from the womb of its mother, into a new world of the Qur'an and Muhammed's leadership. That is what has happened for the followers of Imam W. Deen Mohammed.

Wrap up their brains

You know, the world that we have to come out of is nothing but a world of wrappings. So, they say, "He has risen". The one who was captured, crucified, put away and thought to be dead, he has risen. The proof that he has risen and he is not dead, are the wrappings." He is not wearing them anymore. He left the wrappings that were on his head. That is proof that he has risen.

Now behind Mr. Fard, the Honorable Elijah Mohammed and Malcolm X, an articulate spokesperson for what the Honorable Elijah Mohammed was bringing to the black man and the world, how do you destroy that influence on the new black man? You have to wrap him up, again. "So, let us create a generation of rappers so they can wrap the blacks up, again; and we like what we see in them, what they are hungering for. Let us free it so they can become popular leaders and reach the public like Malcolm was doing for the Honorable Elijah Mohammed. Let these new generation of rappers reach the public and as for their intellectual potential, it is not going to be able to express itself, except through a wrapper. So, the womb for the delivery of their life anew will never be touched, because what we are putting on their brain is just like a wrapper on their sexual organ. So, when they screw their public, they will not produce any babies."

This new mind set is a rapper (wrapper). Isn't that what we are seeing? They cannot carry the intelligence of the black people forward. All they can do is give you a climax that cannot reach the womb. They are wearing wrappers. You see how the Satan gets into our culture?

Knowledge born in man upon observations of objective world

G_d has put His signs in His works. So, there are people of first knowledge, pronounced in Qur'anic Arabic, "Uluul al Baab" (not in the Qur'an only, but in the world). It is the knowledge born in man upon his observations of the objective world. That is their first knowledge. So, the people of first knowledge they apply it. Their instruction was to apply it, not just have it. "Do not hoard it and feel some kind of security because you have it and others do not have it. Apply it. Use it in the world".

So, what we call the exact sciences, or the scientific world, is the world that got the light and applied it. They are using it and benefiting the world of man and society with what they have. They make it work in the world and they are so advanced over the spiritual world that they have lost patience with the spiritual world; and some of them have separated perception from spiritual matters, or from G_d. They say, "You can only perceive what is possible for you in this material world. Forget about this that these other guys are busy with. We are supposed to be the leaders in the world, not leaders in some hidden zones above the people's heads, in the sky."

Subsequently, they have divided the world into spiritual and material, secular and religious and it looks like they are the bad guys. However, the worst of guys is the one who aspires to rise up upon the air or the breath of the earth and set himself up in heaven in G_d's stead. He wants to get up there and take the position that the people see as the seat of G_d. He wants to get up there and take that seat and show himself as G_d.

Religion is where you find the Satan

Now, if we just look at religion as it has presented itself in the history of man, religion is where you find the devil, the Satan, the oppressor. Satan comes in different sizes according to Al-

Islam. There is the little Satan, the middle-sized Satan and then there is the big Satan. So, in the material world or in that realm for the interest of man, the bigger Satan, the big Satan is the one that aspires to get up to the seat of G_d, sit on that seat and present himself as though he is the G_d.

The figure of Jesus Christ as a white person

Now, the figure of Jesus Christ as a white person, if that is not the worst thing that the world has done, tell me what is! To put G_d in the image of the race that works for dominance and uses racism to suppress people, to oppress and hold back one people and to free and advance another (the white and black races), that is the worst thing. If that is not the biggest crime and the worst crime against G_d and religion, tell me what is.

―――――――――――――

Editor's Note: A few years after Imam W. Deen Mohammed became the leader of the Nation of Islam (led by his father, the Honorable Elijah Mohammed, from 1933 to 1975) he directly addressed the negative effects of racism in religion by establishing the movement called C.R.A.I.D. (Committee to Remove All Images of Divine). After a brief time, Imam Mohammed discontinued C.R.A.I.D.'s activities. But, an advertisement expressing the essence of the movement's work continues to be published in the weekly publication, *The Muslim Journal:*

With G_d's Name, the Merciful Benefactor, the Merciful Redeemer

Out of Respect for Man's Creator
A MESSAGE OF CONCERN

By Imam W. Deen Mohammed

What would happen if people would sit in churches throughout the world for centuries with the image of an African American man as the savior of the world before them? What would this do to the mind of the world's children?

What would happen to the world's children put under a figure of a particular race presented pitiable and in pain, "The Savior of all men"?

Qur'an, Chapter 3, verse 64:
"Say, 'Oh people of the Book! Come to common terms as between us and you: That we worship none but G_d; that we associate no partners with Him; that we erect not from among ourselves, lords and patrons other than G_d. If then they turn back, say you, 'Bear witness that we (at least) are Muslims (bowing to G_d's Will)'."

Civilized nations should want that their religion be also civilized. False worship is the worst form of oppression. We are no gods. We are only men, *"Mortals from mortals He (Allah) created"*. (Qur'an)

3
Racism in the Culture

Let me share with you something that happened to me. I was shopping near one of the better high schools on Chicago's Southside. I like to get a little piece of penny candy every now and then, an ice cream cone or a rainbow sherbet cone. When leaving the store, I overheard one bright young lady say, "In the U.S.S.R., basic necessities are free. Russians do not have to pay for education or housing." Moving along slowly with them, stepping in front of them, I turned my head and said. "The Libyans do not have to pay for basic necessities, either". I added, "But you know, there are some things I like to pay for, myself!" A young man turned, looked at me and asked, "What kind of thing do you like to pay for yourself?" I was praying for that kind of response. I answered, "I like to pay for my freedom myself."

A special freedom
A freedom that emerges, dawns, in the very deepest recesses of the soul of man, in the phenomenal spirit of man that ties us to one and the same personal and environmental human concern, is a special freedom. So, being, myself, stirred by that special freedom, I understood something and having that understanding of it is why I said that to those young students. When we start to respond more to the urgency deep within, instead of just reacting to the rhetoric, statistics, research, data, etc., of our preacher politicians and demagogue leaders, we will have that same influence driving us to move out of excessive dependency on others. We will have that influence driving us into personal responsibility and community responsibility for our own circumstances, for our own good future.

Religious-based racist ideas

Setbacks occurring in the cultural processes of life are sometimes so devastating that nothing short of a genesis, one with which man, nature and social purpose are united, can move that people out of that devastating situation into a better life and a better future. For the task of successful living, the African American people must have this kind of genesis. It was attempted by many before us. It was attempted in the social reform work of the Honorable Elijah Mohammed, who led the Nation of Islam. It was not in his racist talk. That was only a reaction to the white man's racism and the white man's traditional religious-based racist ideas.

Many of us have forgotten that the belief that blacks were created inherently inferior received support from ignorant church people and church leaders who said that we were Ham's children; and that Ham was cursed for laughing at his father's nakedness. The Church taught that the curse fell on his children who were cursed to be black. Having experienced cultural setbacks to the extent of social devastation in the life of the African American, we must dwell here on this particular concern; a concern for the establishment of a philosophy for the African American people. African American people must establish a philosophy of life, a philosophy of group behavior. They must dwell there in that sacred unity until the hope is realized by them as it has been realized by other people who now are liberated, while they are still gripping and struggling in the spirit for that kind of liberation in the African American life.

As ironic as it may seem, after coming so far from slave and prison camp conditions, with more rights put on the law books than ever in the history of a people struggling for rights, and being in a land that still attracts the desperate to its offer of free spirit, free markets, free competition, the African American group spirit is still detained outside; still not yet liberated. Screaming Cubans have stopped yelling. They seem to be doing alright in Florida. Crying Haitians are going into the sunshine and drying their tears. The newest arrivals, also, new citizens from the Far East, and near East, etc., are putting new blood into the business life of America. By answering a need in their own lives, they are strengthening this nation.

Cruelty after slavery

Black people have to have a movement out of excessive dependency. The reconstruction period put blacks in a situation to be rubbed like salt into the wounds of the white Southerner. We were put in that situation by Northerners to be used to attract Southern rage away from their Northern white brother who had defeated them in the Civil War. They directed that rage to the African American, whom the Southern white man had enslaved. As a result of that, there came a wave of cruelty unmatched, even by the previous plantation cruelty.

A hundred years of lynching and of Ku Klux Klan terrorism lasted even up to the time I was a young man in Chicago. There was a lynching in the Cicero, a community not far from where we were living on the Southside of Chicago, at which they brutalized a young black male only because he was walking alone in their streets during the quiet hours of the day. He was only there doing work. But they did not believe him. They thought that he was just an intruder or a bold nigger who was over there walking in their neighborhood. So, they brutalized him, and lynched him. That happened when I was a young man in Chicago.

Emmett Till, perhaps you remember how they brutalized him. He was a handsome young boy from Chicago who went to Mississippi unprepared for a racial shock and there he displayed mannerisms that the white man of Mississippi in that day could not tolerate. So, they cruelly lynched that boy, put a weight on his body and dropped him into the river.

One hundred years of lynching

We find that behind slavery came the manifestation of greater cruelty against us. That is not to be charged to the Southerners. That is not be charged to the Ku Klux Klan. That is to be charged to the scheme of the Northern establishment that had to protect itself from the rage, bitterness and vengeance of the conquered South. They had to find something to put as a buffer between the North and South. So, they used the Southern African American. They gave him authority and power right after the Southerners' defeat. They imposed martial law and put blacks over those conquered whites, meaning they then had to take orders from blacks who had just recently been freed. That was humiliating. Especially, since those blacks that were put in those positions were not even educated to the psychological factors in that cruelty and in that situation. They were not prepared to deal with the psychological factors. They were ignorantly trying to do the best they could and allowed themselves to be used in a situation that created for them more resentment and bitterness for the race. The result was one hundred years of lynching, a hundred years of terrible, insane cruelty against African American people.

The spirit of the Honorable Elijah Mohammed

As a result, we have to lead ourselves. Who will tell us that? Who will have the courage to tell us that? What social scientist is telling us that? What theorist or analyst is telling us that? You should understand that this man talking to you is the son of the Honorable Elijah Mohammed. He was a tremendous man, a powerful man. He did a lot of wrong in ignorance, but he had great spirit for liberating his people, socializing his people, reforming his people, socially, and giving them dignity and equality. He did not want to do it walking hand in hand with white people. He wanted to do it hand in hand with brave women and courageous men of his own people. And now, out of his loins comes a son of his that actually has no credit from formal schools, except a high school diploma; in fact, a G.E.D. I took the test and got a diploma from the state and I just have three hours in English from junior college.

But it is out of a person like me that comes the vision, the insight, the direction for the people who cannot find it otherwise. And I challenge you. Your Ph.D. degree will not give you the answers. You have to get it here. I challenge all of you. Your Ph.D. will not give you what I am presenting here. Why? It is because your Ph.D. has no provision for the peculiar situation in the African American intellect. But God provides for all.

Suspect the world of pop culture

We who are influenced mostly by the entertainment world are not healed from a tendency that is in all people, but has characterized us in the eyes of the world; the tendency to be silly-minded, to just want to laugh and have fun. We should now look at the world that we are living in and look at our relationship with this world, the entertainment world, the world of pop culture and we should start to suspect it. We should suspect the pop culture.

I had this told to me by several intelligent individuals, college students. One was a college professor, but I experienced this, too. I went to college for a little while, Loop Junior College and another college on the South side of Chicago. This is what they told me. They said, "Wallace". They knew me personally, so they said, "Wallace you know when we go to college the first thing they want to do is direct us from where we want to go. They say, 'You people are naturally talented. You should study music'.'" And that person is applying for chemistry or something. He wants to major in chemistry, physics or some higher science and they direct him by saying, "Oh no, you people are really just naturally talented. Why don't you take music? You will be a great success."

So, we should suspect the culture that we live in that Pope John Paul said is the culture of death. That is one of the names he gave this entertainment world we have. And he called it, also, the culture of drugs and the culture of violence. His language is shared by many organizations that work for peace in the whole world. They say the same thing of our pop culture, that it is the culture of drugs. It is the culture of violence. It is the culture of promiscuous sex. It is the culture of death. Now where did the Pope get this justification to call it the culture of death? We know it kills. It takes our innocent children's lives, with drugs and all the violence and other things. But he called it the culture of death to say the culture of sin. The Bible says sin is death.[56]

The culture of death
Consequently, we should suspect this pop culture, that it is used by those who want to keep people down that are not up; not only black people, all people; so, they do not have to share with too many. There is only so much to go around at any given time, so they want to make sure there is a lot for those they want to help and a little of nothing for those who they do not care about. And they do not care about those who they do not consider enlightened in their idea of what enlightened means. If you are not enlightened in their idea of what enlightened means they do not consider you to even be a true human. They consider you to be animals in human bodies.

They can give you this world of the culture of death and keep you in check, keep you occupied so your real rational life will not bother you and will not demand that you do more with your life in a real rational and material world. So, by being suspicious of this entertainment life that we have, called the popular culture, we will discover that this world is the greatest promoter of behavior extremism and deviant behavior; that is, what we call sick behavior, or going away from the progressive line in the life of people for their development as human beings or as life. Certainly, we can do bad things, get an idea in our minds to do bad things. But Allah did not create us to do bad things. He created us to be free to make free choices, to choose between good and bad and at the same time, we have to realize that G_d gave us a soul and a spirit and a desire in the soul and in that spirit to always make improvements on our life, to do better.

Nature to progress to be expressed in consciousness
G_d has given that to everything He created. Nothing He created was created to stay small. Everything G_d created was created to get bigger and bigger, more sophisticated, more complex, more intelligent and more productive. He made everything like that. The nature He gave to the earth He also gave to that which comes out of the earth. He gave the nature to the earth to produce and to produce more and more, better and better. That is what He gave the earth.

        The same nature He gave the earth He gave to us that were made out of the earth. That nature is in us to be expressed in our consciousness so that we become even more productive and care for the productivity of the earth; and care for an increase in the productivity of the earth; thereby having a much more beautiful and comfortable world than we would have if G_d had not made us like this. So, do not ever blame G_d for your short comings, for your problems and your failure. G_d is the One Who made you to have everything wonderful.

Culture is the dress of a people

Christ Jesus, according to The Gospel, also is to be identified as the, "Second Adam." The Gospel gives the genealogy of Jesus Christ and traces his existence back to G_d. It mentions his mother and Joseph (peace be upon them) and goes back through that lineage. Finally, it says, *"...Who is the son of Adam."* Jesus is traced back to the son of Adam and he is the second Adam, according to Christian theology, or to Christianity, "Whose father was Adam." And it says that Adam was created by G_d. That is what the Bible says, not what I say.[57]

This Adam then, is a type that includes all of us. All of us are descendants of Adam. According to the Bible and the Qur'an, Adam was tempted and deceived to come out of his dress that G_d had put him in. The Qur'an says, *"Do not let Shaitan* (Satan) *deceive you* (speaking to us) *to come out of your dress, as he did your father and your mother in the Garden."* [58] And it does not leave us to wonder about that dress. It says the dress is the dress of righteousness. The Honorable Elijah Mohammed said that his main job was to put black people in a new dress? He said, "My job is to dress you up." The culture of a people is their dress. The spirit and the intellect and the heart are all supposed to work together to develop a comfortable home for us on this earth. And we live more significantly in our cultures than we do in our physical clothing or in the frame houses and brick houses that we live in. Those things are important for us, but they do not change our lives if we get a different form for our housing or our clothing, unless we let it. As long as we stay rooted and grounded in our healthy culture, our culture protects and feeds our life.

Culture should be influenced by morals and ethics

So, in the Christian world, the culture should be influenced by the Spirit of the Gospel. The culture should be influenced by the morals and ethics of the Gospel. In a Muslim society, the culture of Muslims should be influenced by the Spirit of the Qur'an and Muhammed, the Spirit of Al-Islam. And it should be fed by the morals and ethics of the Qur'an, the teachings and the life of Muhammed, the Prophet (the prayers and the peace be upon him). If we have that, then we have salvation for our lives. If we do not have that, then all we can have is a struggle with a sincere will in us to obey G_d and be the best decent human being we can be.

We have a great struggle here because every time you open up your eyes and your ears, you are hearing that that hurts the spirit you want inside. That is a painful way to live and G_d does not want us living that way; to just have a spirit to obey Him and not an environment to protect and make comfortable that spirit. So, Adam is the type that G_d created and set to the right mold for him to keep his life, make great progress and reach the Promised Land through his descendants. But the serpent, Shaitan, deceived him to come out of the dress that G_d had put him in.

Adam met a Word from G_d

Unlike Christianity or the Bible, in Qur'an, we are told that Adam met a Word from his Lord. He didn't stay in that bad condition. Adam met a Word from His Lord, repented his behavior and His Lord accepted him. Therefore, he is not a sinner. It does not say that he sinned. It says Satan caused him to slip from the foundation he was on before that G_d had put him on.

Going back to Adam, the original man, and keeping the focus, when Mr. W. D. Fard said, "You are the original man," he was talking about the man that G_d made in the mold and in the nature that G_d put in him before he was enticed by the Satan to come out of that mode of life. Mr. Fard was not talking about what we thought he was talking about. When Mr. Fard asked, "Who is the original man?" The answer was, "The Asiatic black man." He was not telling you, you are Asians. You know you are not Asian. You are not Chinese. You are not Japanese. You are not those people. He had already established what Asiatic meant in his communication to us. He said, "The whole earth was once called Asia." This is not anything new for a people who are trying to give a myth to give them a sense of beginning for a new history and a new life.

Sense of beginning in myth

He was trying to give the followers a new life, a beginning point, for their history. So, he said many things. He said, "This happened in the beginning." It is myth. Do not think the Romans had it any different. All people get a sense of their beginning as a civilized community in myth. And the myth when translated, reveals great knowledge, great truths and you can see the reality of it. You match it with its reality and it gives you a higher sight, a higher knowledge and a deeper insight into your life and where you should go with it. So, do not underestimate the power of myth to project people and motivate them to go forward with their intelligent life for community life on this earth.

Culture develops naturally upon human nature

When you study Adam in the Bible, Adam was deceived out of his righteousness, deceived out of his culture that G_d created him for. Culture should develop, naturally, upon the excellence of human nature. That is how culture is supposed to develop. But Satan, the devil, he creates the culture for us and imposes a culture of violence, a culture of death, of drugs, etc., on us. And that culture works against the original excellence of the human nature, retards that and pretty soon you have self-destructive boys and girls; like we have in our streets and in our homes; and crazy, irresponsible mothers and fathers, like we have in our towns.

Adam made to be free

Adam, he was deceived by the serpent, the Satan, the Shaitan, the devil, and from his loins his descendants came and they were not protected anymore. But, they had choices to make. They were free. G_d made Adam to be free, to make choices and G_d made him to have descendants, children, who would be free to make free choices. So, they did not have to stay in bad shape. They were able to make free choices, choose the best and follow the best as Allah tells us, *"And take the best thereof."* [59] Always go after the best. If it is the Qur' an, go after the best, because if you are not right in your heart and you want some wrong, Allah will blind you when you go into the Qur'an. You will think you have something to help you do wrong and you will be doing wrong thinking you are getting help from what you read in the Qur'an. That is the punishment of G_d on you for having bad intentions. It (Qur'an) is guidance only for the, "Muttaqeen," those who reverence G_d and that which He has established to be respected.

Other People before Adam

The descendants of Adam became the industrial people, not others. Some would ask, "What others were there? If G_d made him, there were no other people." The Bible says that the son of Adam (Cain) met the people of Nod, city of Nod.[60] Who were they? Who were the people of Nod? You know what nodding implies. That is what the Bibles says. So please have faith. Do not treat me like the people of Moses treated Moses. If he did not say what they heard in Egypt, they did not want to listen to him. But Egypt oppressed them. Isn't that ridiculous? Some persons, if I do not say what they believe from the world, they do not want to believe it. They doubt it because they did not get it. You know what they have done when they take a position like that? They have doomed their own selves to not get any further than they are.

Deformed by their own world

If what you have could help you I would not have to say what I am saying here. But you are going to hold onto what you've got if I do not say something that agrees with what you have. That is regretful. In the Bible, the book of Genesis says Adam's descendants became the industrial people, workers in iron and other metals and builders. They became very industrious people. Industry grew and grew and their environment that they created could help them or set them back. It is the same today.

The environment that they created caused them to give all their attention to material development. The point is that materialism poisoned their souls and they became so deformed by their own world that they created that G_d punished them with a great flood and the flood took all but a few, i.e., Noah and his family. This is the Bible.

No superiority of white or black

And from Noah came a new development, a new trend, a new world order after Noah. It was the order of the spiritual that followed behind the order of industry. There is great wisdom in all of this and I wish I had more time to explain. But perhaps another day, maybe. Maybe I will write more books and make them available. I need to do it, too, because it burdens my mind that we have this and are not giving it to enough people. Other people can benefit greatly by what I am saying right now and perhaps they would appreciate it more.

Prophet Muhammed, when he gave his last sermon, he addressed issues of today. For example, he emphasized that you have to treat females right. You have to give them equal opportunity for education, etc. If we were addressing this issue right now and did not say where it is coming from, wouldn't we be on time? Yes. And he said, "Treat your servant like you treat your own child. Feed the servant with the food that you eat. And dress the servant with the clothes that you yourself wear." He was speaking on things that we can talk about today and if we did not use his name or did not connect it with Al-Islam, the people would cheer us. Christians, they would cheer us. He also spoke out against nationalism, narrow, fanatical nationalism. He said, "There is no superiority of a non-Arab over and Arab and there is no superiority of an Arab over a non-Arab." Additionally, he addressed color-based racism. He said, "There is no superiority of a white over a black and no superiority of a black over a white." That is what he said.

Kush was the leading nation on the earth

Now who would think that one day blacks would be in a position to be told they are not superior to whites? It was not back there in his time; maybe a couple of thousand years before him in Africa, because at one time there was a great civilization called Kush. It is in the Bible, too. They were the leading nation of people on the face of this earth. They were blacks from Africa. They gave medicine, higher knowledge and sciences to the world of that time.

And Allah does not leave us without mentioning that to us. He says, *"And G_d is the One Who revolves the blessings to the nations."*[61] Again, He says, He tries a people to see how they will they do if they were put into power"; and behind them He replaces them with another people and tries another people. That is the way of G_d.

Developing the intellect of man

When G_d gives the story of Adam in the Qur'an and in the Bible, G_d is giving us a story of our own human life and its capacity and potential for building life not only for itself and its people; but for building life for the whole human world, i.e., cultural life, industrial life, all of it. In Al-Islam, we are to focus on the whole life of mankind, not just on the spiritual features of man or an aspect of man's life. No, we should focus on the whole life; life and all of its wonderful possibilities. G_d created every human being to wake up to that life, to engage that life, to follow the best leadership, to take us forward in that life or to that life; to assume responsibility for taking our world or our people into that life. That is the Promised Land.

It was mentioned to Abraham, why? Because Abraham is the second father. He is a second father representing the coming of concerns for developing the intellect of man. Abraham is the one who focused on the intellect of human beings and wanted to unite the whole people; because as the Bible said, he will become a father of the nations. And the Qur'an says G_d made him to be a leader of the many.[62]

So, he represents the attention to intellect, to improve the intellect, to study the sciences and his discovery of G_d begins with him studying the objective world, the world out tnere. The story in Al-Islam, the Qur'an, goes like this: Abraham left his father. His father was the biggest man and his society was the most advanced society at that time. He left his father because his father believed in idols and he didn't believe that his father should have people believing in idols; not that he thought his father was stupid enough to think that an idol made by their hands of clay or something had power. He knew better than that.

But he just wanted to show him how ridiculous it was that they worshiped idols and gave that idea to others who were not as educated or as developed, intellectually, as his father and the ones who were running the society. The masses, the common people, were actually thinking that those physical things had divine power and they feared them and prayed to them. This was the sin of taking advantage of the ignorant, the unlearned. That was a great sin that bothered Abraham. So, he left his people, his father's land and he traveled among many people. We should study him, also, in the Bible; how he never would take advantage of anybody. If he could make it by himself, he did that. If you helped him, he wanted to pay you back. That is Abraham in the Bible.

The beginning of higher education

He represents this new focus for man's advancement by cultivating the intellect, not the physical world. So here is education. It is the beginning of higher education, the beginning of the attention to the need for higher education. It comes with Abraham, peace be on him. So, he was sitting as a thinker. Thinking on G_d is the greatest. The Qur'an tells us, *"Think for thinking profits you."* You will benefit by it". In Arabic, it is, *"Wa la dhikrul-laahi akbar"* and it says, *"And the best of thinking and reflecting is the thinking on G_d.*[63] In our efforts we have done all we can with our spirit and spiritual life. We have spirit and working to serve our spiritual life has gotten us to be involved in the outer world and has connected us with nations, with national leaders and with top people in other religions. But, look at how small we are in our material structure, these little small places we have. Even I, the leader, have a little small, crowded space to work in. The people I am meeting, it is not suitable for me to invite them to those places. They are not used to coming to a man of my popularity. I did not use other language because some are so sensitive. "You heard what he said about himself? Let somebody else say that." You are welcome to say whatever you want to say.

A house for the human spirit

They see that we are advanced so far up here in our spirit and in our heart, but we have nothing to really give a home to that advancement. Where is the material home for our advancement? We do not have it. G_d gave us a spirit inside of a flesh body. G_d does not put you in a world with a spirit and no flesh body, although they call us spooks. G_d does not put a spook in the world. G_d puts the human being with a flesh body in the world. He gives you a house for that spirit and G_d speaks of communities, towns, neglected, their roofs falling in and He speaks of their restoration. He says, "It is as though it was a resurrection." What is G_d telling us that for? To tell us that He creates us with a spirit and a flesh body that houses us and He made his container nice. In Arabic, it is, *"Fa Ahsana suwawakum,"* translated, *"He made beautiful and nice your physical description or your physical picture"*.[64]

Guidance for your community life

He is saying that to tell you, "Now you are living with your body on the earth and He has sent you guidance, not only for your spiritual life, but also for your community life." And He made everything in the skies and in the earth for you to study and utilize, make use of. In Qur'anic Arabic, it is, *"Wa sakh khara lakum laa fis samaawaati wa maa feel ardi ja'meean"*, translated, *"He has made useful for you, to study and bring into your service for your community life whatever is in the sky and whatever is in the earth."*[65] That is what G_d says. If you register this with your rational mind, your good common senses what I am saying, then right now, you are getting the same help from the Qur'an that the first followers got from Muhammed, the Prophet (the prayers and the peace be on him).

But they were not constipated in the head and couldn't throw out crap. They were not like that. They were waiting for a man who respected their rational mind. They were waiting on him and they heard him and they took charge of their immediate affairs and their life. As a result, they became the people to bring a reawakening to the intellect of man. Scholarly pursuits were revised because of studious men and women seeking to bring utility, knowledge and science out of G_d's creation. That is what happened. The same thing is going to happen here.

A help in the whole world
It is going to take a long time, but it is going to happen, because those who are already on these college campuses are going to more and more be looking at what Imam W. Deen Mohammed, the son of Elijah Mohammed, is saying. More and more they are going to be looking at what I am saying and they are going to take it to heart. They are going to do just what the first followers, the intellectuals in the following of the Messenger of G_d, Muhammed, did. They are going to do just what those followers did. They are going to make this community beautiful and productive, materially advanced. And they are also going to be a help in the whole world.

So, the whole world is going to become much better than it is. That is what is going to happen. The Honorable Elijah Mohammed said, "Islam is freedom, justice and equality." Many of his followers remember him saying that. More than saying that, it used to be on the blackboard in the temple and the blackboard was in view of the congregation every Sunday, Wednesday and Friday. And you would see on that blackboard those words, "Islam is freedom, Justice, and equality."

The unity of all people under One Creator
As Muslims, we turn toward the House, that little, simple, symbolic structure in Mecca we call, Ka'bah, or G_d's House. The Qur'an says it was built for all people. In Qur'anic Arabic it is, *"Inna awwal baitin wudi'a lin nas"*, translated, *"The first*

of the houses, the most ancient of the houses built for all people".[66] That is what is given to us in Qur'an. And of that house, it says, *"That house is full of blessings"*.[67]   Listen to what Allah says to us in Qur'an; not only a blessing. It says, *"And guidance"*. So, after hearing this from me, please do not look at that house anymore as just a simple thing or structure. Look at it as a structure that exudes and sends out messages to the intellect of the faithful that helps them with the Qur'an. That symbol, that sign holds messages to help us guide our life and take our lives forward where Allah, our Creator, wants it to go as a community. It is a community symbol. I have commented on it before and in the future, I hope to comment on it some more. But understand that it is a sign of the unity of all people under one Creator and it is a sign of their G_d given natural, inherent talents, potential and ability to be skillful, to be creative, to be productive. It is a symbol of that. It holds that. It is a symbol holding that message for all of us; for all human persons.

Man originally one nation

If you except what I have said, then you can understand better what Allah is saying when He says, *"Wherever you are turn your face towards this house and wherever you may be scattered Allah (G_d) will bring you all together"*, if you accept the message by and in that symbol". [68] That message says, *"You were once one people."*[69] You were not different nations. You were not different races. You were once one people. G_d made you all one human type that is given in Adam, human. G_d made you all to be human in your excellence; human, spirited and motivated by your excellence that He created you with. That is the human that G_d made. If you respect each other, that all of you were made that way, that will bring you together. That is what Allah is saying. If you respect what he is saying, G_d tells us that He made all of us like that and all of us to have equal opportunity to achieve based upon our inherent qualities and properties as productive life.

The pursuit of happiness

The founding fathers they could never have envisioned this great society we have here if they had not come into that kind of knowledge or insight and it is given in these words. "We hold these truths to be self-evident that all men are created equal and endowed by their Creator (recognizing the Creator) with certain rights that you cannot take away from them." Government cannot take them away, inalienable rights; "Among these, life (the right to live), liberty (the right to be free to progress), and the pursuit of happiness." And they translate this in the Constitution to mean the right to vote.

First, it was the right to have property, your own material property and upon that you had the right to vote. That was done away with and it should have been done away with. Poor people do not have anything, but, they should have the right to vote, too. Everybody has to have the freedom to have their say so and influence the state and course of our government. So that was changed.

According to the Qur'an, G_d reveals to the earth. It says, *"And the Earth shall behave as though G_d had revealed to it"*;[70] the earth. Now what is that in reference to? The Bible promised that there is coming a time when light is going to light the throne and the light is going to spread from the throne and cover the whole earth; and the whole earth is going to be lit with that light. Again, he Qur'an gives it by saying, *"And the earth is going to behave as though G_d revealed to her"*; the earth, itself; the whole earth.

Promised Land is community life

Allah says to us in the Qur'an, *"You are the best community, the best society, evolved, brought out of darkness and corruption for the good of all people."* [71] That is what Allah tells us in the Qur'an. That tells those who have studious and alert minds that Allah does not accept that we just have faith. But we have to establish community life. If G_d came to us shouldn't we be able to do as much as any other people have done? You either believe it or you do not believe it. If you believe that this is G_d, the Creator of everything that has reached us now and is guiding our life, then we are supposed to have something in our future as big as any other people have in their future. That means we are supposed to have sciences, medicine, industry and cultivation to offer as a benefit for the whole life of mankind on this earth. We are to have that and no less than that. That is the Promised Land. It never said Promised Ether. Ether is up there. It is heavenly gas. It did not say Promised Ether. It said Promised Land.

Dust off his feet

The New Testament says that Jesus Christ would shake the dust off his feet. You cannot have your material interest carried by the wind. You have got to protect it. Do not let it get light out there somewhere. The wind will blow it away. But it means more than that, though. Jesus Christ said he would knock the dust off of his feet. It means if they reject him he will leave the town. It says, but pity on them if he knocks the dust off his feet. It means he was lifting up the people who did not have any material establishment. They were like dust and could be blown or taken away by the breath or by the spirit. So, if they were not going to let him carry the dust of the people, of the poor and ignorant people, he said he would knock it off, leave them there with them; and it would be worse than Sodom and Gomorrah what would come behind him.

What religion does

Yes, that is what religion does. True religion goes after the suffering people and tries to take them off of the ground and put them in a better position to make something out of their lives, do something with their lives. And if you prevent that kind of a messianic leader, or that kind of preacher from doing his work, then that nation will be threatened by those people, that element in their society and eventually, it will cause their downfall. The spiritual teacher, he gathers the poor people. They respond and he gathers them and they are like dust on his feet. His foundation was not dust. His foundation is spirit. Jesus Christ was the Spirit of G_d and a word from G_d. So, his spirit is very strong and also with the spirit is faith; faith, spirit, and the word of G_d which guides him. That is in the foundation. But now if he goes out of that foundation and the dust goes away and is left back there with the people, then they are in serious trouble. And that is what the Bible is saying, that his coming and taking up the cause of the poor and the ignorant people is what spares great nations and great powers; and it does. But they have always had a way of managing the spirit crowd, or those people who have spirit but no knowledge and guidance.

"Why have you struck me these three times?"

The ancients have always had a way to contain them and hold them. Balaam is one of them. And you know Balaam was riding the donkey, until the donkey saw an angel with a flaming sword, or a messenger with a flaming sword, or with the Word of G_d that is like a flaming sword; a sword that lights up. And it does not only cut, but it lights. It is a light, also. It cuts and slays, but it is a light, also. That is the Word of G_d. So, the donkey saw an angel holding a flaming sword in the pathway, in the way that it was traveling with its master on its back and the donkey, said, *"Why have you struck me these three times?"* It says he spoke with a man's voice, not a donkey anymore. The donkey spoke with a man's voice and he said, *"Why have you struck me these three times?"*[72]

People not to be ruled through psychology

Now that is answered in the Abyssinian, Bilal ibn Rabah, in the time of Muhammed, the Prophet. Bilal was a slave and he was refusing to obey his master. That is asking his master, "Why have you struck me these three times? Why have you put my whole future in slavery, my flesh, my mind, and my spirit?" His way was just to protest slavery and for doing that his master put him in the hot sun and Jesus was put in the heat, too. So, they put Bilal in the hot sun and then put a heavy stone on his back and they thought that that would make him break and decide to give up his interest in Prophet Muhammed's call to Islam. But when he could not speak, he just held out one finger. He was so miserable he could not even speak. He just put up that one finger, telling the one who insisted that he believe in more than one G_d, that he still believed in one G_d. He said, "Ahad, only One".

One day donkey will speak as a man

Finally, one from the Muslim side, a friend of Prophet Muhammed, Abu Bakr, came and paid his ransom, which shows that the master's interest was in money. The reason why he had a slave as a slave was because a slave was giving him money. So, when the money came in a big enough amount he gave up that slave. After all, he had lost him anyway.

Bilal is actually the answer. Prophet Muhammed knew this. He is the answer to the Scripture that portrays the poor and ignorant people as a donkey and that one day the donkey will speak with a man's voice. So, the call to Islam does not accept that the people be ruled through their spirit or by psychology; but that they be free to be educated; that education is the answer.

Nafsil la amara

But the problem started way back in the time of Noah. Noah had three sons and Ham was Egypt. Ham was the one that showed ignorance. He wasn't uneducated, but his character was that of nafsil la amara, the compulsive self, or impulsive self. So, the impulsive self could not handle human conditions, intelligently, laughing at the condition of the person rather than responding to the need in that person. The other two brothers responded to the need in the person. That was their father, Noah. But Ham did not. The Bible says he laughed and the curse fell on the children of Ham. That only means that if that disposition, that silly disposition, gets into people, it is going to be passed on to their children. Isn't that what happened? The way the poor, ignorant people behave, when they have children their children come up behaving just like them, until one rebels, until one sees a way out of it or sees that it is wrong. His character is too strong to take it and he leaves it. He then departs from his parents or his society. But in most cases, it is passed down from parent to children like that.

A scheme to pass behavior down

That is why African Americans, blacks, were called the children of Ham. That is exactly what they were saying and the curse was on them that came upon Ham. It wasn't going to hit them right away or directly. But that disposition in him would carry on and get worse and worse. In those who came after them it would get worse and worse, meaning it would grow. If you accept that kind of disposition in yourself, it is going to grow. You're going to pass it on to your children and in your children it is going to become worse and that will be a curse on the children of Ham. But look at who they call the children of Ham, not the Egyptians. They call the children of Ham, the Canaanites and the Church used to sing about Canaan Land. Do you know who Canaan is? Canaan is translated, "A dog, the dogs, canine". Yes, Canaan Land, the children of Canaan.

The Egyptians were highly educated and they were the most advanced of all of the nations in the time that the Bible is addressing. But the tendency to find fun in things is in all people. So, they pointed this out and said that Ham had this tendency. Now you know Africans are a jolly people, most of them and it is going to pass on down to a people lesser in progress or in development as a people. It is going to pass on down to them. You know what that tells me? It tells me that they were going to see that it is passed on down to them. It is a scheme to pass this behavior down to the lower class of people who actually have a territory that they call Canaan Land.

Black folks marked early for enslavement
In Arabic, it is called, Kaina'an, but it is Canaan, the same Canaan and it would be passed down to them and mark them. You see how early they marked black folks, African black folks for enslavement? So, they said, "It will not hit you, directly. It is going to hit your descendants. They are more vulnerable, so it is going to hit them. They are not scientific-minded, or science-minded like you are. It is going to hit them and they are going to become the hewers of wood and totters of water for their two brothers", Shem and the white man, Japhet. Ham is Semitic and the other one, Shem, is Semitic and one is the white man, Japhet. They gave the highest place to the white man. But, the white man did not do that and he is going to be knocked down, later.

It is Jafar, in Arabic, but it is Jephat in the Bible. But there were three of them. One is Ham. That is Africa, representing the Semitic African like Ethiopia, that is still identified as Semitic. Then the other one that is given most credit to I think he is Jafar and he is white. He is the white man. He is of the white race. So those are the three races that they saw back them; one black, one brown and one white. Now the white one, the Prophet called, red. He didn't call him white. The Prophet called you by the way you were affected by the sun. If the sun makes you black, you are black. If the sun makes you red, you are red. If the sun does not change you, you are white. And the white person, the sun doesn't change them. It just messes the skin up and might even destroy the skin. But, they are still white. So, he called them red, the red man. The Arabs, lately, here recently in our history in maybe the last 30 or 40 years, they do not translate the red man as red. They translate it as white. But when the Prophet said there is no superiority of a black over a white, he didn't say white. The word was not white in Arabic. The white is red. He said there is no superiority of a black over a red, nor red over black. The only superiority is in obedience to G_d.

Blacks not only ones put down
Now when the world was really oppressive they put people from Africa in slavery in the West (America, etc.) and degraded us. But we were not the only ones. There were others that were treated the same way by their people. They have been pushed down, too. The Polish people have been rejected by the world, most nations and they treat them like they are not worthy of respect. You go there and the country is in bad shape. They are way behind the rest of the European countries, especially Great Britain and they are way behind us, too. When I went over there Poland looked like the United States when I was in my early teens, i.e., horse drawn wagons, etc. You can still see them on the streets, the people looking like they are on welfare, or suffering. I mean by the way they dress and look. This was war

time I am talking about, World War II time. The people were carrying a great load. There were only a very few having a good life.

Need for messianic leadership is gone

So, the whole world was in bad shape like that. Now the world has changed. You do not have strong nationalism anymore because people accepted that they have to live with one another. They have to live together. They have to cooperate, trust each other, benefit from each other and help each other. So that is the attitude now in most nations. You do not have this sharp national line separating people anymore. When that was the case there was still a justification for messianic leaders; not only that. In the past, the biggest problem for black people was that we were rejected, socially. Nobody wanted to socialize with us or have us in their social environment. That social rejection has gone. You can go in some of the smallest towns now, South, North, East and West and everywhere and you can find blacks all mixed up with whites, all in the same area. So, to put it succinctly, nationalism and racism is what made it necessary for messianic leaders.

Now, that is not of much consequence at all in our lives. When there was virulent racism or nationalism the messianic leader was necessary. A messianic leader comes to save a people, not all people. Every messianic leader of the past that I know of was in the Bible. They are not in the Qur'an. It did away with it.

4

Racism and Reconciliation

Don't you know that the so-called black man's flesh is white? It has been scorched on the outside, because while the so-called white man was living in the north region out of the direct rays of the Sun, he could not get browned by the oven. But black people were living in the tropical zones, right under the direct rays of the oven and it took about 50 billion years to make them black toast on the outside. Haven't you seen the black person get cut by a razor and it opens the flesh up and it is white? You are only black on the surface. You are white under the skin.

The Book says, that is, the Bible says that Ezekiel, the Prophet, was told to prophecy to the dry bones. It says, *"Son of man, prophecy to these dry bones in the valley."* [73] I thought about that. I said, "Good G_d, Almighty. Oh Lord, I have been wondering how to convince these people." Look at how simple this is. It is as plain as day. We are told that when Gabriel blows his horn, that we are going to stand up out of our graves, and according to Ezekiel's words, the bones are going to stand up. It did not say flesh. In fact, the book says that flesh cannot enter the kingdom.

Resurrection must restore humanism

It is a necessity that the knowledge that G_d originally designed in human nature for man to grow up with must be restored to him; that he must be given back those human principles that will uphold his flesh. That will make his environment safe from racism. From color consciousness. He must return to human principles; principles dictated from the very substance, from the very design of his true human nature.

Every man and women is black in original nature

"And who is this man, this natural man that G_d made from the very beginning whose conscience tells him the right steps to make in life?" That is the original black man. "Why do you call him black when you say that all men are accepted before G_d?" All men are black when they are in their original nature. "What is this strange terminology that you are using today, W. D. Muhammed?" It is the true understanding in the Bible. It is the true understanding in the Holy Qur'an. That is what I am talking about. This is not my language. This is the language revealed to the Prophets by G_d and I am telling you that Almighty G_d says in the Bible and in the Holy Qur'an that every man, every woman, is true and black if they are in their original nature.

Human nature teaches to follow right road

What does it mean to be black? Black means to trust the life that G_d put in you from the beginning. To trust my human nature, that is being black; to trust the voice of my moral nature that tells me not to lie; that tells me not to mistreat people, to trust the voice in my natural life. It tells me not to short change my brother because he is not of my flesh; to do right by everybody. I do not need any Gospel to tell me that. I do not need a Torah to tell me that. I do not need a Holy Qur'an to tell me that. Before the Torah, before the Gospel, before the Holy Qur'an, I was told that through my human nature. Human nature is what taught me to follow the right road, to follow the road of truth and justice and turn away from the road of lies and injustice. The human being tells him that. What do we mean when we say that particular, original being or original nature is black? We mean that we do not get knowledge. We get feeling. This is not coming from the pages of knowledge. This is coming from my nature, from my own being. It is coming from the mystery of my own creation. Yes, that is Melchizedek.[74]

Every human being should remain black

That is the ruler that was even before Aaron. That is Melchizedek, the natural life that G_d created for every human being; that life that dictates that he rises higher and higher in moral excellence, virtues and principles of excellence; that his knowledge lifts him up, but obeys also moral guidance. That life is the life of the original man. That is the original man. Should we remain black? Yes, every human being should remain black. We are created black. We should die black. What do we mean by that? We move from the blackness of original nature to the blackness of faith. Is faith white? No, faith in us is black. Faith means that I follow whether I see my way or not. I follow because I believe in G_d. We must return to the original nature of the human being. The color of that according to Scripture, in Scriptural terminology, is black. We must also develop from that base a faithful man under the dictates of G_d. The color of that faith, according to the Gospel, according to the Book, according to Revelation, is black.

What does the book say about our first teacher? It says that your first teacher was fear. What color is fear? Fear is black. Can any man live without fear? No. Then no man can live without the black man. Fear G_d. Remain black. White man, I am calling you today and asking you to please remain black. Though your skin be white, remain black. Fear G_d and trust your human nature.

Black stone in corner

The black stone in the house at Mecca, in the Ka'bah, is the cornerstone. What does cornerstone mean? It means the stone that every other stone is aligned by. It is gauged by the cornerstone. You place the cornerstone according to the measurement dictated by the master builder. That is G_d. Once that cornerstone is in its place, according to the direction given by the Master Builder Who is G_d, then you line every stone up in line with that cornerstone so that the wall will be on the square. And when you have a perfect square house you have a house that belongs to East as much as it belongs to West; belongs to North as much as it belongs to South. You have a universal house when you have a house built perfectly on the square. And what is that stone that can line a building up so that when it is finished, it belongs as much to East as it belongs to West, as much to North as it belongs to South? That is human nature, for human nature is one and its color is one, i.e., black. What does the Scripture say? The Scripture says the light of this world is darkness with G_d.[75] Then the original nature that we call black in this world, if they accept it, it will be white. If this world will accept our blackness, our blackness will light up the world.

Government and religion work together

Pharaoh is pictured in the Bible as a wicked oppressor, but, every Pharaoh was not like that. I studied ancient Egyptian history and some of their leaders were very good. Some of the Pharaohs were very good for their people. All of them were not like that. It was just one in that period of time. The Pharaoh of the persecution or enslavement of Moses' people, he depended on very mysterious, symbolic religion to hold the masses of the people. He had a priesthood that worked directly with him in the government to control the people.

Do you know government and religion work together in the ungodly world to control the masses? That was in the time of Moses. I am not saying all churches. I am not saying all leaders. I am not saying all government people are like that. But there is enough support among the church leaders or religious leaders, today and enough support in the government to keep that thing going. So, they have an alliance, a pact. They work together to keep the masses ignorant, babyish.

Education: The greatest tool for advancing the society

We cannot get where we want to go and get people where they should go if we just pretend that we do not see these things. We have to inform the people. Education is the greatest tool for advancing the society. But do not think that education is always in academia, in public schools, or in the schools established for the people. No, it is lost many times. The main help for the intellect or for the mind of people is lost many times because the world decides education. Do you know the big developers, the big investors in industry control government and education? We only see opposition to them when a bright intellect appears somewhere in the country for a group of them. Usually, it is a group because a bright intellect is not going to be happy by himself. He is going to have to find some companions to work with him.

So, it turns out to be a small group of people who get together and then challenge what is going on. They point to the problem and they expose it or they seek to get it changed and if they can't get it changed, then they expose it. Then we see change for the better in the academic world or in the political, governmental world. We see change for the better. But it is not going to happen without an interruption. Somebody has to go into to this who are attentive to what is good for the human public and what is bad for the human public.

Old must be replaced with new

We have reached a point for our growth as a people on this planet earth, as communities, where the old must be replaced with the new. This old way of controlling the masses and managing the public has to be done away with and I know some of you are guardians and they have given you a small job in the establishment. So, you always think that you know more than your leader. You think that they have given you something higher than what G_d has given your leader. Well, that is your privilege. I am telling you, you can go back and tell your bosses the day is out. It is a new day.

We cannot continue to treat grownups in our public and in our neighborhoods like there is no respect for their brains and their intelligence, like they are no more than babies. We have to respect the adult mind because Allah will interrupt your thing. The change is now moving from appealing to the emotional side of life to appealing to the rational side of life; the land. That is what Jesus did when he said, *"Come from the waters and follow me. I will teach you how to become fishers of men"*.[76] That is what he was saying. That was the leadership. Tell me how many he was talking to? How many did he bring from fishing? Twelve. So that is the leadership. How many are in the President's cabinet? Twelve. That is the leadership. So, he was calling the leadership of that time.

Fishing the waters of human life

They were fishing in the waters. They were fishing in the waters of human life, not a lake. They were fishing in the waters of human life, human composition, the sensitivities. Your sensitivities and sensibilities, both are in the water. Sensitivities means feelings and sensibilities means the ability to sense in your nature. But if they play it from the waters all of the time and do not address you as a land creature, you will lose your land; that is, your nature to respond. You will lose the rational ability to respond, as I said earlier and you are just tuned up to respond, emotionally.

"Let me get my manual on Negroes"

The individual life of one person that is the key. The life design and pattern for one person is the same in nature for every other person. Do you know when you go to a dentist he does not say, "What is your race. Do you have any other races in you before I start this procedure (drawing blood)? Do you have any other races in you? I do not want to make a mistake if you have some Spanish blood in you." No, the human being has human blood and pure, real, true science is universal. It is the same everywhere. So, a doctor can treat anybody and he does not have to say, "Wait a minute. Let me get my manual on Negroes." The science is all the same. The science of your hair, your skin, your blood, your teeth, your bones, all of the sciences are the same. That is the work of the G_d Who made you. He made all of us the same so that we can be doctored on without a whole lot of unnecessary problems.

Where is black religion?
When it comes to teaching religion, too many want a Negro religion. They say, "Give us a black religion!" Where is that black religion? I do not want that one". Well, let us take out that which does not hold up when tested by truth and science and G_d's creation. Let us take that out of it so it will be a religion for all of us. Let us take the white lord out of Christianity. Isn't that what G_d says to the Prophet? He says, *"Say to them. Let us come to terms that respect us equally; that we raise not from among ourselves lords and patrons other than G_d."*[77] Do you think the Qur'an is not addressing racism here? That is what it is addressing. Now you have a white looking man who belongs to a specific blood line for a race or a group of people and you have given us that type and told all of us that that is our G_d, our lord. The Qur'an addresses that in many ways and when it says, *"Let us come to common terms that respect us equally"*, it is addressing a lord that you make and it serves your psyche to make your psyche super. But if you give that same lord to a black man in Africa it will regress him.

Again, the Church has to change. Our African American church it has to change. They have to change. We have a lot of help on our side from Christianity, now. Recently, a well-known priest said, "There has to be some fundamental, major changes in Christianity, if Christianity is to survive". I cannot tell the Church that. I cannot tell the black Church that. I cannot tell the Baptist Convention that. They are not ready for that. I cannot tell the holiness people that. They are not ready for that. But, why can't I tell my students and people who say they follow my leadership? Why can't I tell them that?

Stand up in your own souls

When I say this to some persons they become dead. They die right in their seat. Their thoughts are not moving. The blood has slowed up. This is many African Americans. But, we can change. That old stuff that they ingrained in us, we can get it out and stand up to it. You have to be able to stand up in your own souls. Do you know that? That is what it means that Christ stood upon the water. He was an original man. He could stand up in his own soul. But the average one of us, if the soul gets disturbed, we are drowned by the water.

You have to stand up in your own soul. You have to stand upon truth in your spiritual life and as well as in every other form of life. Stand up upon truth, whether it is against your own feelings or not. And you have to change your feelings and fight your feelings. You have to have a battle with yourself. Isn't that the teachings of Muhammed, the Prophet, that the greatest jihad (battle, struggle) is the jihad with your own self?

A boxer has to train for a fight. He has to get himself into condition for a fight. This is a jihad. You have to train your soul, your psyche, your feelings, your sensitivities. You have to train your waters to support truth in the face of challenges from the world. Coming together as faithful people should answer

G_d's call. It has to be a training program to put us in the condition necessary to be successful against the challenges. Once we get our own life together and we feel confident that, "I am organized. I am self-composed for the job at hand, internally", then, we are ready to join those who are similarly constituted internally, to get the big job done.

We only need a few

You may say, "Brother Imam, you have a job on your hand." We only need a few. I think it was Margaret Mead who said, "Only a few are needed, together, well organized and they can change the world". [78] The world has been changed by a few well qualified persons coming together. The world has been changed by a few and she said, "Not only has the world been changed by a few, but that is the only way it has ever happened." So, you never should expect that a multitude of people are going to respond to the call of G_d or the call of the Prophets. Do not ever expect the multitude to do that. They are going to sit and listen and go back and eat Kentucky Fried Chicken, Popeye's, or Burger King hamburgers, etc. and watch the football game or the soap operas. And they will be the same people they were before they heard Imam W. Deen Mohammed.

A bond to unite all people

Dear beloved people, Prophet Muhammed is said to have told some of his followers and left it for the coming generations that no one would enter Paradise except on the order or design of Adam. The Holy Qur'an says this and Prophet Muhammed also taught us that Adam represents the common ancestral origin for all people. By study we have come to understand that Adam represents the basic human qualities and the intellectual and moral potential of every person; that human dynamism, or driving force that says, "No", to anything that stops short of giving man his full due. If we cannot enter the Paradise except on the order or pattern that G_d established Adam on, then we should understand from that that here is given a bond that can unite all of us together.

Our good conscience has no more faith in us

Adam does not represent the worldly man. Adam represents our original nature and our original nature does not willfully disobey G_d. Our original nature slipped because of confusion in the environment. Our minds are taken off course and pretty soon we find ourselves following a course that is detrimental to our original nature. The original nature is not responsible for that. The true human conscience is not responsible for that. We are fighting the true human conscience to put those things over until we reach the point where the conscience has no more faith in us. The conscience does not even listen. The conscience does not even complain because we have for so long ignored the conscience that the conscience has lost faith in our minds ever conforming to what is right. So, we blame it on what G_d did. But it should be blamed on the habits that we formed.

Dear people, this is the key. This is the key for bringing people of good will together and it is the key for bringing Muslims together. Why? It is because Muslims also lose their original posture. The Arab will become so much involved in his Arabism that he will lose his human posture to a nationalistic posture. That happens with the Nigerian and with the Sudanese. That happens with the Egyptian. That happens with the Pakistani. That happens with the man from Kuwait, from Iraq, or from Iran. It happens with all the people, because they forget that we have been formed upon the original pattern of man. And we are to question ourselves as to what is right and proper for a human being, not for a black man, or a white man. We should question ourselves as to what is proper for a human being; not for a Jew, or a Muslim per se. It says of Jesus, *"As long as I am in the world, I am the light of the world"*.[79] But once the original posture leaves the world it is no longer the light. Then, narrow interests come into the picture, greed, nationalism, racism, etc. and man is taking off his human clothes of righteousness.

Hung up on black

Black people have become hung up on the term black. "Oh, I am black." We do not say, "African". We say, "Black". Black is more important than African, now. "Oh, we are black people". What is that saying? That does not say much, i.e., you are a black person. What do you mean when you say you are black people? Do you mean you are the human beings that survived slavery in the South and all that? Well, say it like that then! That means a lot. That says a lot. "We human beings who were put down lower than animals, called monkeys, or inferior humans, we have survived all that to be present in the leadership of America in these great times and bad times". Say it that way, then. But just do not say you are black. What does that mean? Nothing. You are just black. That is nothing. They have black Indians and they are blacker than you. They have black Asians and they are blacker than most of us. Most of the black ones they are blacker than you. So, you want to see your superiority in black skin? Go to Asia. Go to India and you will see that they are blacker than you are.

Black superiority is reverse racism, a trick of Satan

So, our problem is this hang up we have on color, on black. That is the trick of the Satan, to use the white over you to make you go in the reverse, or to the other extreme, copy his logic and use of black. He is superior. He is white. So, you go and reverse it for yourself, but using his logic. You say you are superior. You are black. That is the scheme of the Satan and Satan has lost to Al-Islam as preached by the son of Elijah Mohammed. Satan has lost.

We think of our identity as a race and we are occupied by thoughts of our identity as a race, or our identity as people of a culture. We have our own culture or we are a people of soul. We have our own soul different from the soul of other people. Our own spirit is different from the spirit of other people, as a group. A group has group spirit. Members of a group they have the group spirit. Members of the group they have the group soul. Members of the group, they have the group cultural taste. So, we do have a distinct life that is more than just our color. We have a distinct life that makes us different in the human picture than other people. That is all true. But we should not make those descriptions of ourselves more important than the one Allah mentions and reveals in the Qur'an. He says He is the One. G_d, the Creator, He is the One Who gave us our different features or pictures when we were in the bellies of our mothers, forming us as a life in our mothers. And we come out with the features of our mothers or our family, father and mother. He said He gave us that.[80]

Human picture most important

If you belong to a black family or African family, He is the One Who gave you your black picture. It is created by G_d. It is the creation of G_d. G_d is saying, "I am the Creator of all your different variations of colors and features going across nations and also among yourselves in your own family. I am the One Who ordered the way you get your picture, the way you get your features and your colors, etc." G_d is saying, "I gave you that". G_d is saying that to say, "I gave you that so you are approved in that. I approve you in your racial identity. I approve you in your national identity", etc." But G_d says what? He says He is the One Who gave you your features or your pictures when you were in the in belly of your mothers, in Arabic, *"Fa ahsana suurakum"*, translated into English, *"Then He made most excellent your single picture"*.[81] What single picture? The picture you have in common with all people; the one that is more important than all the rest; your human picture.

He is the One Who made you most excellent. The word in Arabic is, "Ahsana". It means, "Better in quality, better in worth, better in performance". It is just the best. Now what if you put all these other descriptions with it, like you take a hanger or structure and you want to put other garments on it? You want to put the garment of racial identity, the garment of ethnicity on it. You want to put all these garments on the raw structure, or the first structure. They will break down that first structure and they will all be lost as trash. But if you make the first structure right it will be strong and it will hold up all the others you put on there.

The mold of human sensitivities

So, we should be finished with the identity hang up. We know what G_d wants for us in terms of how we are to view ourselves and how we are to relate to one another. G_d wants us to understand that the creation that He made first, is the best for us. He made us human in our souls. He gave us human intelligence and He does not want us to ever get out of that mold, the mold of human sensitivities and human intelligence.

As long as we stay in the mold of human sensitivities, pure, excellent, human sensitivities and we respect our human intelligence, we are safe for other life. Allah didn't give us ape intelligence or monkey intelligence. He gave us human intelligence. As long as we stay in the mold of life that Allah created for us and gave to all of us the same, the common human creation that He gave all people on this earth; as long as we stay in that mold and appreciate that life, then we are safe for all the other developments.

G_d gives us answers for all our needs and if we are believers, G_d has revealed all the answers in His Qur'an for us. And He has revealed in Muhammed, also, the answers we need. His creation is really Revelation for us; the creation of Muhammed, himself, as is the mystery of Jesus a Revelation for us.

For each is an interest

We do not have unity and the more we talk about it, the more disunity we get. Our leaders, our preachers, are all taking about the need to have unity and as I said, the more they talk about it, looks like the more disunited we become. So, we are not making any headway following those who have been leading us. It is as plain as day in the Qur'an how we are to keep our unity, how we are to perceive our unity and keep it. It is plain as day.

G_d says, *"For each is an interest that is turning him"*. The word is, "Wajh" and it means, "Your individual interest". Isn't your face a window or a mirror that we look into and we can see your interest? So, the "Wajh", is called, "Face". For each is a face G_d turns. It is not face, really. It is, "Wajh", but it is a play on face. So, the interest comes from the term, face. It says, *"For each is an interest by which you are being turned...Therefore, turn your faces towards this masjid"*. [82] What is it talking about? Majid Al-Haram. It is talking about the masjid at the Ka'bah. That is the masjid it is talking about.

"I love you in your race"

That masjid at the Ka'bah is a masjid for receiving all nationalities, all the different people in world who are Muslim. There, all the different colors and nations come together and they have prayer together in that masjid that is called, Ka'bah, the most ancient of the houses for the worship of G_d. The Qur'an says wherever you are G_d is saying I approve you having your individual, localized interests. That is what G_d is saying.   Look at how wonderful G_d is. He is solving our problem and He is bringing it to our souls. He is saying, "I love you in every mold I made you in. I love you in your color. I love you in your race. I love you in your tribe. I love you in your national picture. But what is more important for you is the first picture I gave you, your human picture." The Qur'an says, *"So for each is an interest."* I will have interest in culture, interest in science, interest in whatever, business, etc. I will have my own personal interest. No matter what our interests are G_d approves of all of these interests as long as they are decent and of good intent. Nothing natural has G_d denied you. Whatever He has made you naturally He approves of that.

The human excellence intended for all people

So, can we talk about African Americans as Americans and say, "Oh, do not mention black. Do not mention any credit to the race"? This is not Islam. Muslims have to keep that out of Islam. You are wrong. G_d wants us to see the beauty and excellence of all our pictures. But what saves us is that we hold on to the common identity with all people and that is the most important identity. I keep repeating, that is the human identity in the human excellence intended for all people by G_d. G_d intended that for all of us, the excellence of human nature.

So how do we get our unity back? How do we solve our problems with race? G_d says, *"So turn all of you your faces to this house."* That house (the Ka'bah) symbolizes the unity of all people upon the pure human nature and excellent human model that G_d made. That is what that house symbolizes. That house is a sign, a symbol for the unity of all people from Adam, all the human race. That is what it is a sign of.

The Qur'an says, *"If you all turn faces towards this Masjid wherever you may be scattered,* G_d promises, He says, "I will bring you together."[83] So, G_d has promised that He will bring us together no matter how far we have been scattered. No matter how distant we are from each other, He will bring us together. And all we have to do is turn our interest back to the common human life and human excellence that G_d created in all people or for all people, even if they have not expressed it, or realized it, yet. That is what G_d says.

Human excellence better than racial excellence

How can anyone's race or his interest in his race hurt him if he accepts that human excellence is better than racial excellence, that human excellence is better than national excellence? Those things will become weak and corrupt if you do not build them upon, or establish them upon human excellence. *"Lift me up and I will draw all men unto me."*[84] That is Jesus Christ in the Bible. *"Lift me up"*. Lift up the human excellence that G_d intended for all people. Lift it up for other people to look at *"And I will draw all men up to me"*.

No one ascended to heaven but those already in

In the Bible, it is read where it says no one has ascended to heaven who was not already in heaven. So even going to heaven must be an experience realized on this earth in these natural circumstances. And if you do not achieve it in these natural circumstances you will never achieve it. That is the Bible. Man is deprived of his complete evolution, for lack of a better word right now. He is deprived of his complete vision and his perception is limited. He is held back from realizing his complete, full possibility for perception, vision and understanding in this world. What holds him back is incorrect delivery of G_d's word. They do not deliver it, correctly. So, by not delivering it correctly man loses the way that G_d created for him. I said, "Created".

Go back to the religion of origin

So then, to bring man back, he has to go back to origin or back to Eden. What is Eden? Eden is his first conception or his first awareness of his existence as a thinking being in creation before man made anything. There was nothing man-made. There was nothing he could point to as his own work. That is going back in his thinking to origin. So that is what you have to do. You have to go back to the religion of origin, the origin upon which G_d structured man or fashioned mankind, society and everything, men and women, too. He is not able to do this without G_d's guidance. He cannot find his way and G_d's guidance is always close. In the Qur'an it says, *"If my servant asks about Me tell him I am near"* [85] As close as your creation, that is where His guidance is. Also, in the Qur'an Abraham said, *"The one who created me shall guide me."* [86] He said, *"All of these other gods are my enemies, except the one Who is the Lord of all of the world's; the one Who has evolved all mankind"*; not just one nation or one people; but all of them; all the worlds.

So that means Christ Jesus as misperceived in Christianity is our enemy and he has done more damage to black people than anybody else, because they have used Jesus on us more than they have used him on anybody else. During slavery, "Remember Jesus loves you." During the Klu Klux Klan era, "Remember Jesus loves you." Now we have the terror of moral corruption besetting all of us, but nobody is saying, "Look at this serious problem and 'Remember Jesus loves you'."

We are not making it too well through this terror. The black man is not making it too well; not through this terror; the terror of moral corruption and moral death. No one is pointing to Jesus to tell us, Jesus loves us. If they would do it, it would save a lot of us. They would say, "Look at how we are giving ourselves to a life absent of moral sense or moral interest. The young people and the old people are joining each other in vulgar displays. You see this test on us and if you look at it and really register the whole thing, it will bring tears to your eyes. But remember while you are looking at it, Jesus loves you. It is not what he wants for you". And who is this Jesus? It is the Muslim in us. It is the Christ in the Christians; that original nature; that original innocence that will save us; that can save us all the time, always. G_d does not change the condition of the people until they change what is bothering their souls.[87]

Christ is salvation

So, they mystify the power of our own souls to deliver us from the world's problems, free us from the world's problems. They mystify it so much that you think it is not possible for you, that you are hopeless. Christ is salvation, meaning that Christ is in you. Your savior is in you. You are created with your savior inside of you. That is what Christ said, *"I in the father and the father in me and I in you and you in me"*.[88] And Muhammed said, *"Say to them I am a mortal just like you."* [89] "Whatever is in my soul is in your soul", that is what it means. Whatever is my true nature, is your true nature.

This is a language of deliverance and salvation. And it can save us and any other people who are under the world's darkness. It can save all of us but the mystifying does not help at all. When they arrested Jesus what did he say? "Why do you arrest me in the night when everything that I have done was in the day?" [90] So, the Qur'an comes. What is the Qur'an? It is the clear understanding for the clear report given. The Arabic word, "Mubeen", means, "Very clear, perfectly clear; openly expressed, not secretly expressed".

No problem is too big to solve

So, the answers are all clear and no problem is too complicated or too big. The Qur'an says, *"He shall level the mountains"*. [91] The mountain is symbolic of a lot of things and one thing it is symbolic of is mystery. The wise man is on top of the mountain. The Wizard of Oz must be up there, too. G_d said He is going to level the mountains and they say now, "Level the playing field." Do not rig it against anybody. Be fair, that is what it means.

In a very strong hadith taken to be very authentic, Muhammed, the Prophet, said G_d offered him the way to carry out his mission through the mountains or through the plains and he chose to go through the plains. This tells us that he is one of those figures who level the playing field or level the mountains. But then it was necessary because G_d says, had He not placed mountains on the earth then the area would have not been stable and it would have brought down society's structures or left man's world in ruins. That is what it means. [92]

Ocean symbolic of the collective soul

So, there is more than one picture of the mountain. Some mountains are high but have no snow. They are in hot regions and they ascend very high. They are luxurious and they have an abundance of beauty and value exposed; whereas, some mountains are just rocky and stony. They are not supporting vegetation, life or whatever and all of them, as they ascend so high their tops are very cold. If they ascend high enough, no matter where, it could be in Africa, or anywhere, the tops of the mountains a very cold. But look at the mercy in that. Being cold like that, they collect water that turns to ice. They collect and they store clean, good water and when they experience warm times the water melts, runs down the mountain and becomes rivers with a mission to relieve misery in suffering society.

Our aim is to become oceanic

Where are these rivers headed? They are headed for the ocean, the lowest spots on earth. So, all that is on high shall yield, in time and let its purity go down to the lowest of the low and is going to end up depositing itself in the ocean. The ocean is symbolic of the collective soul, the biggest body of water, the biggest spirituality that you can find and what is that? It is man's common soul. That is where all people come together, all spiritual instances come together. Therefore, our aim is to become oceanic, not little small lakes and rivers. The oceans do not exist without salt and salt leaves a bad taste in your mouth if you get too much. You want to rinse it out.

When mankind comes together without discriminating against people because of race and national origin or anything, what are we doing? We are registering the burden on the human soul and we get a bit salty, don't we? We say we have to organize and change things. Allah loves that, too, in man's soul. That is why it says in the Qur'an, *"From the sweet water and the salty water you get delicious meat"*.[93]

We should meet in ocean of souls of mankind

This language is so beautiful when we free ourselves. As long as we are in the prisons of our own narrow thinking, we cannot see the full beauty of G_d's Revelation. But if we meet in the ocean of the souls of mankind, we can see it there and those creatures in the ocean they move about in a serious fashion. You do not see the big fish and whatever, in an ocean, moving about like they are going to a carnival or to the playground or something. They move around like they have serious business, like they are seeking serious business. But those little playful fish, sweet water fish, they are just flipping around and about. By contrast, in that big ocean, the big creatures are moving with cautious precision. If you have not seen them, go to the aquarium and you will see the difference and how they move.

Definite purpose serves unity and reconciliation

Some fish, like salmon, when they go to spawn they are headed in a definite direction and they continue in that direction until they get there. So, what it is saying to us is that there must be a higher purpose in the intellect of man to keep or to hold his intellectual vision where he does not lose it and have things distracting him and to bring unity to his life. Purpose brings unity to our life. When you give yourself to a higher purpose it serves to unify your intellect where your intellect is not going this way and that way and every way. So, a definite aim or purpose serves the unity, serves reconciliation. A better word in this expression would be integrity. It serves to bring about integrity for man when he has a higher purpose and integrity of conscience where his mind has something to protect and advance his vision going forward and his thoughts for his vision go, advance forward and in harmony. So, it serves to unify or bring about integrity for the human being's intellect and consciousness.

Agreement in a definite focus

Integrity means wholeness, but it also means, harmony, agreement and a workable unity. That is very important for productive minds. It has to achieve a higher purpose, something that appeals to the mind's need for peace, harmony and integrity. It means agreement in a definite focus. A person of integrity is a very strong person because something higher has formed order, has contributed to their mind coming to order and having a vision, a definite plan and a commitment to not violate the principles for the plan. Stay moral. Stay rational. Stay focused. Stay obedient to a higher cause. That is what makes great people and, eventually, a great society.

What Scripture wants in the human being

That is the intent in religion and Scripture. It is not always respected in religion as expressed by preachers or leaders, but that is what Scripture wants in man; to find the higher cause that can bring about the best order for his intellect, for his mind and situate him as a thinker, or a visionary to accomplish all that G_d created man to accomplish on this planet earth.

Muhammed, the Prophet, wanted to see all of us reach that when he said to his followers, "Meet me at the water pool."[94] The language used is like a big bath tub. So that says that his mission was to bring us all together for a refreshing bath. In the Qur'an, it pictures him as the unlettered Prophet mentioned in the books that came before, really mentioned in the Torah and the Gospel. And what is his mission? It is to purify you and to free you from every yoke or bond of slavery. All that enslaves the mind he came to free us from it.

A taste of death

The Scripture says, *"You shall have a taste of death". Every soul shall have a taste of death.*[95] G_d gives death and what is the death that G_d gives? If G_d gives death why does He want us to die? As the serpent told Adam in the garden, *"You won't really die. Your eyes will come open".*[96] So why does G_d create us and then leave us in a world that is going to bring death to us, eventually? So, our eyes will come open. Experience death means you are going to become conscious of this death, taste it. You are going to know its flavor. It is a bitter pill. I believe it has hemlock in it to lock up my social movement in my system. You see, myth and religion go together. Religion and Scripture reflect the wisdom of myth.

So, did the Greek philosopher really get locked up in prison, physically and did they really give him hemlock and he died? No more than Jesus was put on the cross and they gave him vinegar and he died. The Qur'an answers it. It says, *"No, you shall have a taste of death"*.[97] If a person can taste something, they are still living. It did not say it was going to kill you. It said you are going to have a taste of death. It did not say death was going to kill you, "O Death where is thy sting?" So, we have to die to the mind the world gives us and come into the mind G_d created us for.

They locked up his social movement

In Scripture, the scholars are depicted as cows and a yoke is what they put on cows. So, to take the yoke off means to free the intellect of the scholar, because false religion persecutes the scholars. The philosopher (Socrates) was imprisoned and then they gave him hemlock to execute him, to kill him. It does not really mean they killed him. But they locked up his hem (social movement) and that caused rigor mortis in his blood that feeds his brain and his whole body (students/scholars). That is hemlock. What is hemoglobin? It is referring to blood and a woman who was a sinner on the ground, she didn't feel clean enough to even stand up before Jesus. She just stayed stretched out on the ground. She touched the "hem" of his garment and was healed. The hem of his garment forms a wide circle. But that wide circle is down there low at the feet with the common man. She touched it and was healed. She understood his social mission, that it was for the common people. It came all the way down to her. A sinner was healed and as that song says, "How sweet it is."[98]

The motor city

For Black people in America, the healing from the wounds caused by racism, slavery, Jim Crow, etc., began in the Motor City, Detroit, Michigan, in the early 1930s. The man who started it all was not from America. He was a man of mystery as mentioned earlier in this publication and his name was W. D. Fard. Fard simply means a person whose real name is not known, like when we say John Doe or whatever. When he came to Detroit in his own planned role, I don't think he was that serious about the role he played. He came in the role of the second coming of Jesus Christ, but he was coming to black folks. Everything was made black.

What he formed or established, i.e., the Lost Found Nation of Islam in the Wilderness of North America (Nation of Islam) has been called a black cult by the press. A man named, Father Divine,[99] was already teaching something about black gods and he was making Jesus black. He was a big Christian preacher. I am trying to give you the environment he (Fard) came into at that time, in 1930-1933. He left in 1934.

Noble Drew Ali and black Masons

Additionally, there was a man named, Noble Drew Ali,[100] who was also a black man, or African American, as we say now. He thought he was preaching Islam. I don't know, perhaps he did not think he was preaching Islam. But he was preaching a brand of Islam that was strange. He did not have the Qur'an of the Muslims. He gave his followers a little pamphlet of maybe 50 pages and he called it the Qur'an; but it was not the Qur'an. They called themselves Muslims and they traced their ancestry back to the Moors of Africa. They were also in Detroit, Michigan, in the poor area or the slums, and were decent people from the Church. But they were kind of a unique group, too. Some of them were black Masons. There were also females (Eastern Stars) who belonged to the same kind of idea like the black masons.

As I said above, Mr. Fard came in the role of the savior, Jesus Christ or the son of man. He always mentioned himself as the son of man and my father (Elijah Mohammed) became his student. He placed him in charge of the following when he left the states after about three years and went back home or somewhere. We don't know exactly where he went. I suspect he went to the Fiji Islands, but we don't know that.

I am sure he influenced my father to rent an apartment on the second floor of a house that was on Yemen street and I was born in that apartment. I have to say a little bit about him selecting that place. Now, understand that he is a guy that was hiding what he was doing and my father was a preacher. My grandfather's name was William Poole and he had his own small congregation of Christian followers in Georgia where my father and mother were born. Mr. Fard chose Yemen Street and I am sure had my father live on this street for a reason.

The Supreme Wisdom

The Yemenites, even now, are not an accepted people. The Northern Yemenites are kind of dominating the southern Yemenites and it is believed that the Yemenites had a great civilization at one time. We believe that Queen Sheba was their leader. You perhaps know the story of Solomon and Queen Sheba.

There were a lot of contradictions in the papers called, *The Supreme Wisdom of the Nation of Islam*, given by Mr. Fard to my father, Elijah Mohammed, to preach to all the black people he could attract from America or from the Christian churches. In these supreme wisdom papers, you could see the magical way that Mr. Fard was converting them. I mean he had some powerful magic. He called it magnetism that was attractive to the black person who was dissatisfied. Mind you, he came to the worst part of Detroit, where he knew people were having bad times. He was looking for those who were discontented, not satisfied to be identified as Americans, or as citizens of America. They did not feel they had citizenship. He came to attract them. Those were the discontented and if they were discontented somebody was saying everything they liked to hear, especially about being put down like a lot of blacks were put down at that time.

Putting ourselves down

Actually, today, I think we are putting ourselves down. When you have been put down and dissatisfied so much, i.e., you have been called, nigger and black, etc., so much, you don't even like the term, black. If someone calls you black from your own African American community you want to fight them. That was the sensitivity at that time. If you wanted to get a fight with any African American person, just call them black; even call them nappy-headed. It would almost get you into a fight. But calling someone black sure would, right away.

The things that protruded out of those papers as contradictions are many. I will just mention those that caught my attention and disturbed me even as a child. One was, "The black man is G_d and all righteous". We know that is not true. The other one was, "The superior people are not the white race, but the black race. The white race is a race of devils made or grafted out of black people by a black scientist named, Yakub". Yakub, in the religion of Al-Islam, is Jacob, who is a Prophet. When you read the Qur'an, there is nothing like that about Jacob or Yakub.

Lastly, I want to share with you how I started to break with the idea. I recall being left at home by my father and mother. We had the first house we ever owned in Chicago, a frame house on 6116 Michigan on the south side of Chicago. My father was coming down the steps. Sometimes I would be up late doing my homework. I believe it was almost 10 at night and that is the time the meeting at the Temple was usually adjourned. He is now leaving the house. My mother was following him and they were all dressed up like for the Sunday meeting.

He said, "Son, your mother and I have to go to take care of some business. We are going to be gone for some time and we want you to stay here with the house." This was on Wednesday night at the Temple. I accepted but I was a little afraid, because it was night time. We were never left at home by ourselves. I had sisters and brothers. Some of them had gone off and gotten married, but I still had three or four brothers and one sister and they were not at home. They were also out for some reason. I cannot even recall the reason they were out, but I am sure it was something that my father and mother accepted or approved of.

So, I am there in the house by myself. My parents left and I finished my homework and I am getting very sleepy. I am tired. It was a time in the season when the nights got very cool. So, the night is very cool now and the house is starting to talk to me. Upstairs is talking. I am hearing noises. I am down stairs and after a while I am hearing sounds in the basement that sound like a group of people having some kind of party down there. They were talking, laughing. I am hearing all of these things and I am afraid. It was so real I had to go down and check the basement.

I went down to check. I was very afraid, especially, when I saw images of a big table in the basement and images of people who looked very old; mostly men. But I think a couple of women were at the table. They looked so old that I felt like if I had struck at them dust would fly off from them. There was white dust on them.

This was the actual picture I saw. I had been taught not to believe in anything but materialism and material reality. We did not even believe in a spiritual life other than the life we have on this earth, now. I think a sect of Jews also believe the same, so this is not anything new.

Better future as a people in America

Mr. Fard put all of these strange things in our life and in our minds to overcrowd our minds and load it with things that did not agree, did not gel, so that it would pressure us as we got more education to wonder why this was done to us and to either leave it abruptly and say, "I am through with this", or say, "The man was a good man. I believe he came to help us. So, let me see why did he did this. Let me see if I can find some answers in what he did".

So that was my situation and after differing with those teachings I met many members in the following of the Honorable Elijah Mohammed and I know that they, too, overlooked those things. But they stayed with it because they thought it was sincere and it promised us a better future as a people in America and in the world.

I am going to include here what I did that I believe started me on my spiritual journey. We did not pray in the traditional Muslim prayer form, the formal way of praying for Muslims throughout the world. We only did what is called dua' and it is not prayer. We called it prayer, but in our Islam, it is dua', meaning, calling on G_d; the individual just calling on G_d. I went back upstairs, but I was afraid to go to bed. So, I put my hands up and I said, "Oh Allah, if I am not seeing You correctly will You please let me see You, correctly? Ameen." I strongly believe that G_d answered my prayer.

A word environment to contain

Now, I have told you a little something that I think will help you see that we were certainly a strange creation in America and we have made a long journey out of the maze of that esoteric, symbolic and satirical language teaching environment.

It was a word environment to contain us that would be so attractive to a people who did not know themselves; did not know their past and did not know why they were put down like they were in the United States of America. It was prepared for us so we could work our way out of that maze and as I said, G_d was with us, obviously, and we did work ourselves out of it into the mainstream of Muslim life in America and the world.

Mr. Obama's effect on African Americans

As for the broader black community of America, I think the healing is going to be more difficult, because whether we admit it or not, white people had the white church and black people resented that and how they were put down. So, black people formed a black Church. I am talking about black Christians. They call it the black Church. I think it is going to be very difficult, but I do strongly believe that Barack Obama's historic campaign for the presidency, bringing people together and identifying not as black people, only…has positively affected blacks in America. In time, I think it is going to affect blacks in Africa and all over the world.

The history of blacks and whites in America is a powerful history. In a speech on race during his presidential campaign, Mr. Obama hinted that the roots of racism go way back and I know the roots of racism go back to ancient cultures and the myths and the mythology of the world. What contributed to us being separated as whites and blacks and having this serious race problem is the belief that G_d made it and intended it this way and He (G_d) said the black man should be put down.

Slavery and racism from misinterpreted story of Noah

As I referred to in chapter two, some small, religious Christian groups have read into the story of Noah and his three sons an idea that supports white supremacy and slavery for blacks.

Maybe you don't know the story of Ham. I have to make sure you know the story.

Noah had three sons. One was Ham and he was the one who showed that he had a silly mind. He saw the nakedness of his father, Noah, who was drunk. This is the Bible.[101] He laughed at his father. His other two brothers did not. One was disgusted. He turned away and one was really the ideal, real loving son. He saw his father like that and he covered his father. He put a cover over his father, but Ham laughed. It says the curse did not fall directly on Ham, but on the descendants of Ham and the Bible says Ham is Egypt.

Noah's sons not flesh, but dispositions

I don't know. I cannot understand how the Canaanites are the descendants of Ham. They are not the genetic descendants of Ham. You have to see it in political history. That message reached us more than it reached white folks. They saw to it that that message would reach black people in America. We heard that we were called the children of Ham and that we were cursed. The curse didn't fall directly on Ham. It fell on the descendants of Ham, or the children of Ham, called Canaanites. The Bible says they were cursed by G_d to be servants of their brothers, white people. That is how we understood it and the Bible says we were destined to cut wood and carry water to them, to do the little cheap jobs of servants.

So that is in the Bible and I know, as a student of religion, you are not supposed to read that story like that. But why is it put like that in the Bible? I know the three sons of Noah are not even flesh. They are dispositions in the spirit and soul of human beings. So really, all the family of man have these three figures in their souls. Perhaps that is too much for some to understand, but I think I had to say it.

A mercy to the whole world

Muhammed, the Prophet, the prayers and the peace be upon him, was an Arab. He was an Arab born in the city of Mecca, the blessed, holy, sacred city of Mecca. When he formed the leadership he didn't just have Arabs around him representing the leaders. He had Persians looking like white folks. He had Africans like Bilal, his companion. These were all his number one companions, like Jesus Christ's disciples, peace be upon Jesus Christ and upon Muhammed.

Prophet Muhammed had his companions who were like disciples. In fact, we could say they were his disciples; the same. They were for him as Jesus Christ's disciples were for Jesus Christ, peace be upon the Prophets and they were Arab. They were Persian. They were African. Salman was a Persian and the record says he was white-skinned. He was white. So here is a man that G_d chose for the world, but not because of his race. He was commissioned to be a mercy to the world, not just to his race. And he demonstrated that by selecting or accepting that the leaders closest to him represent the colors of the human race; not Arab or one race, but the human race, the family of mankind.   Black brown and white were in his immediate staff of people.

We say we are his followers. We are in America. Should we be trying to keep our leadership one hundred percent black? If we do, we are not following Muhammed's way. We live in a country that is mostly non-black. So, if we are going to live in this country and make progress in this country, we should demonstrate to this country, to the American people that we are not hung up on race. We should demonstrate that we truly follow Muhammed, the Prophet, the servant and Messenger of G_d, the Seal of the Prophets, the last of them.

When we do that we show the unity of mankind and we defend ourselves, protect ourselves from being charged with racism. Racism is not permitted in Al-Islam. Racism is too far from the nature and beauty of this religion to have any closeness to the important works of this society. No, we must abandon it. We must put it on the outskirts of our life and activities and not permit it to come into our borders, again.

Racism is for the devil

Racism is for the devil, not for us. Let the devil have racism. He wants to divide the races, to weaken the family of mankind, to set it against itself. We aren't going to help him. We are going to defeat him and we are making great progress. In fact, the devil is retreating. He is shrinking, becoming smaller and smaller. His smoke over Los Angeles is going away. He doesn't build big fires anymore. We have got him on the retreat. That was just a recognition of your progress for the environment.

Picture of mankind seen in one family

Al-Islam is a religion of unity and its central idea is unity, oneness, called tauheed, from the word, "One". Tauheed is a derivative of the word meaning, "one", in the Arabic language. So, the central idea is tauheed and that tauheed is the essence of Islamic teaching and life. It is what gives birth to our kalemah, our creed, "La ilaha illallah Muhammedan rasullah. There is no god except the one G_d (Allah) and Muhammed is His Messenger." Tauheed (unity or oneness) is expressed in this language or in these words, "G_d is One and His creation is one universal system or one systemic whole".

That means the whole of the creation, whatever you see in the sky, whatever you see down here on earth, water, wind, fire, whatever the masses that float in the sky above our heads, stars, moon, everything, all of them are held together by one universal law; and they are not really foreign to each other. They are elements in common. They have elements or constitutions in common. Similar elements make up their constitution. The earth has a hundred and something elements. These same elements that are in the earth, that make the earth what it is, can be found up there in those bodies, too. They are up there in the heavens, too.

The gases that we have down here can be found out there, also. It seems as though there was just one creation of elements and gases and they were spread out over the whole world, the whole universe, the whole existence of things and we find them in all the things strung throughout the universe, sky and earth. This tells us that this was made by One G_d. That is the conclusion the great thinkers came to. That is the conclusion that the great thinkers came to thousands of years before our time. They said, "Oh G_d, we behold Your handiworks and we know that You have done these things." They did not say, "We know that You and Your buddy did these things." They said, "We know You have done these things", because what they were observing spoke of one Artist, one Designer, One Maker, One Creator. Praises be to Allah (G_d).

One family, one humanity, different colors
So, this tauheed expresses in a statement that G_d is One, the world He created is one systemic whole and the family of man is one family, one humanity, though we are different colors, features, spirits, cultures, tastes and different behaviors; just like the children of the same parents differ. Two parents, mama and daddy, can have thirteen children and we will find some of them preferring some things that others reject. We will find some of them with a certain taste for clothing. We will find some of them with a spirit that the others do not have. Some of them may be inclined to be humorous. Some will be inclined to

be serious; right in the same family. Some will be lazy right in the same family and some will be devilish right in the same family.

Chiara Lubich, the late president and founder of the International Focolore Movement, put it so beautifully. She said (I am condensing it), "The whole of mankind can be seen in the picture of just a single family". That is true and I have been preaching that for many years. It can be seen in just a picture of a single family.

G_d evolves family to global humanity

Actually, what is being done by G_d through man, but also through the forces of nature, is the progress of the original family life. G_d is evolving the single, family life for the whole of mankind and the single home life for the whole of mankind. So here is the core of man in his original social nature and spiritual nature growing, influencing as it grows, until it fuses into all the children of mankind and brings them into accord with the single soul of mankind, of all people.

Where we are going

Do you know we are many souls, just as many as there are humans? But we are also a single soul, as it was in the beginning. And G_d says, *"As it was in the beginning so shall it be in the end."* [102] We are different souls, but at the same time, we are one soul. And it is that one soul that is going to make a home for all of us. But all of us in our collective life, in that one spiritual life that we call human life, in that one soul, can make a home together. When we conform to it and we become reconciled with it again and conform to its hungers and its thirst, we can have this earth as one home accommodating all of us as one family.

That is the destiny. That is where we are going. The great lady, Chiara Lubich (may G_d grant her Paradise), she saw that with the light of her own Bible, the New Testament, the teachings of Jesus Christ, peace be upon him. We see it with the light of Qur'an and the works of Muhammed, the Prophet (the prayers and the peace be on him), to show us how to live our religion. We see it, too. We are in harmony with Chiara's aspirations for humanity and she is in harmony with our aspirations for humanity. There are many up in the heavens with controls down here working for the same thing and we are not going to fail. We are going to be reconciled as one, global, human family. This is G_d's Movement and you cannot reverse G_d's Movement! We are not going to fail!

END NOTES

All Qur'an references are from the A. Yusuf Ali translation from the original Arabic into English. All Bible references are from the King James Version.

Preface

[1] Woodson, Carter Godwin (1990). *The Miseducation of the Negro*. Trenton, N.J: Africa World Press. Carter Goodwin Woodson (December 19, 1875-April 3, 1950) was a historian, author journalist and founder of the Association for the Study of African American Life. Dr. Woodson was also founder of The Journal of Negro History in 1915 and was regarded as the "Father of black history". In 1926, he initiated the celebration of Negro History Week", which eventually became Black History Month". He also founded the Associated Publishers, the oldest African American publishing company in the United States.

[2] *The Souls of Black Folk: Essays and Sketches*, DuBois, W.E.B, A. C. McClurg & Co., Chicago, 1908. William Edward Burghardt Du Bois was an American historian, civil rights activist, Pan-Africanist, author and editor. He was one of the co-founders of the NAACP in 1909. Dr. Du Bois became well-known nationally as the leader of the Niagara Movement, a group of black activists who wanted equal rights for blacks. He was in opposition to the "Atlanta Compromise" that was presented by Booker T. Washington. Du Bois believed that the

liberation of African American people would be spearheaded by an intellectual elite he referred to as the "Talented Tenth".

[3] Ida B. Wells (July 16, 1862-March 25, 1931) was an African American journalist, newspaper editor, sociologist, etc. and an early leader in the civil rights movement. She was one of the founding members of the National Association for the Advancement of Colored people (NAACP) in 1909.

[4] Washington, Booker Taliaferro, Garden City, New York, Doubleday & Company, Inc., 1901. Booker T. Washington was an educator, author and advisor to presidents of the United States. He was born in slavery and was one of the most prominent leaders in the black community promoting black businesses. Consequently, he was one of the founders of the National Negro Business League. Washington was the founder of Tuskegee Institute in Alabama and author of the Atlanta Compromise that called for African American progress through education and entrepreneurship rather than challenging Jim Crow and segregation in the South.

[5] Mary McCleod Bethune (July 10, 1875-May 18, 1955) was an educator, stateswoman and civil rights leader. She was appointed as an advisor to President Franklin D. Roosevelt. But she is best known as the founder of a private school for black students in Daytona, Florida, that eventually became Bethune-Cookman University.

[6] *Black Boy*, Wright, Richard, Harper Perennial, 1966. Richard Wright (1908-1960) was an author whose works helped change race relations in the United States in the mid-twentieth century. He gained national attention in 1938 with his publication of four short stories called, Uncle Tom's Children. When he published his novel,

Native Son, it was selected by the Book of the Month Club as its first book by an African American writer. In 1945, he published a memoir detailing his youth in the South (Arkansas, Mississippi and Tennessee) and his eventual move to Chicago, called, *Black Boy*.

Introduction

[7] The mysterious man who mentored Elijah Mohammed had many names, W. D. Fard, W. D. Muhammad, Fard Muhammad, W. F. Muhammad, Wallace D. Muhammad, etc. This contributed to his mysterious status among the membership of the Nation of Islam. He actually was from what is today called Pakistan. After meeting Elijah Poole (who later was called Elijah Mohammed) he taught his proto-Islam to Elijah and the followers for three years and then he disappeared (in 1933). Elijah Mohammed eventually moved the central headquarters of the movement to Chicago and functioned as the leader until his death in 1975.

[8] Qur'an 6:32; 29:64; 47:36; 57:20.

[9] Qur'an 5:60.

[10] *Forty Hadith: An Anthology of the Sayings of the Prophet Muhammad*, translation by Ezzeddin Ibrahim & Deny Johnson-Davies, Holy Qur'an Publishing House, Beirut, Lebanon, p. 26, 1980.

[11] Qur'an 26:89; 33:4-5.

[12] Qur'an 21:92; 23:52.

[13] Old Testament, Genesis 2:7; Qur'an 15:28-9.

[14] Qur'an15:29.

[15] Lee, Harper, *To Kill A Mocking Bird*, J. B. Lippincott & Co., 1960.

1
The Origin of Racism

[16] The historical story of the Dravidians and the Aryans outlines the first time in recorded history that racism in religion was promulgated and used as a tool to subdue and conquer a people.
[17] The Ku Klux Klan or KKK is the name of a movement in the United States that has advocated white supremacy, white nationalism, and, at one time or another, violence against African Americans, Catholics, Jews, immigrants, etc. since the 1870s. Ironically, members of the KKK swear that they uphold Christian morality, though virtually every Christian denomination has officially denounced the KKK.
[18] Bible, Genesis 1:1-5.
[19] Qur'an 35:27.
[20] For further explanation, see the history of the Dravidians and the Aryans in the ancient Indus Valley in India.
[21] See Rogers, J. A., *Nature Knows No Color-Line*, Helga M. Rogers, 1270 Fifth Avenue, New York, NY, 1952 and J. A. Rogers, *Sex and Race, Volumes I, II & III*, Helga Rogers, 1270 Fifth Avenue, New York, NY, 1967.
[22] Dr. Joel Augustus Rogers (September 6, 1880-March 26, 1966) was an author, journalist, and historian who contributed enormously to the history of African Americans in the United States. He was one of the greatest promoters of black history in the 20th century.
[23] Qur'an 7:129.
[24] Qur'an 28:77.

2
Racism and Religion

[25] Qur'an 2:193
[26] Ibid
[27] Old Testament, Genesis 11:7
[28] Old Testament, Psalms 2:3
[29] Qur'an 2:34
[30] Qur'an 7:11-12; 55:15
[31] Qur'an 6:32, 29:64, 47:36, 57:20
[32] Old Testament, Deuteronomy 30:19
[33] New Testament, John 3:14
[34] Qur'an 4:76
[35] Qur'an 2:79
[36] Qur'an 40:57
[37] *"Khaaliqum basharam min teen. I am about to create man from clay".* Qur'an 38:71
[38] *"Thumma anshanaahu khalqan aakhar. Then We developed out of it another creature".* Qur'an 23:14
[39] Qur'an 2:29; 23:17; 67:12
[40] Miʻrāj, or The Ascension, in the history of Muhammed, the Prophet, was his spiritual ascension into the seven levels of heaven where he met Adam, Jesus and other Prophets, including Ibraheem (Abraham) on the seventh level and then travelled to Jerusalem.
[41] Qur'an 67:3; 23:86
[42] 1. A doctrine that equates G_d with the forces and laws of the universe. 2. The worship of all gods of different creeds, cults, or peoples indifferently; also: toleration of worship of all gods (as at certain periods of the Roman empire)"- *Merriam-Webster Dictionary*
[43] Qur'an 53:43

[44] Frederick Douglass, a social reformer, abolitionist, orator and statesman, was born in slavery, escaped to freedom and became one of the leaders of the abolitionist movement in Massachusetts. He was perhaps the most influential African American leader of the 19th Century and was the first African American ever nominated for the vice presidency of the United States.

[45] Qur'an 75:2

[46] Qur'an 89:27

[47] Qur'an 12:53

[48] Old Testament, Genesis 9:24-7

[49] Qur'an 21:68-9

[50] Richard Allen was a journalist, educator and religious leader who was born into slavery in 1760 (died in 1831). Eventually, he was able to buy his freedom and went on to found the first national black church in the United States, the African Methodist Episcopal Church in Philadelphia, in 1794.

[51] Qur'an 30:30

[52] Ibid

[53] Qur'an 3:54; 86:15-16

[49] Old Testament, Psalms 118:22; New Testament, Acts 4:11; Mark 12:10; Luke 20:17; 1 Peter 2:7

[50] Old Testament, Malachi 3:8-9

3
Racism and Culture

[56] New Testament, Romans 6:23

[57] New Testament, Luke 3:22-38

[58] Qur'an 7:26-7

[59] Qur'an 2:57; 2:172; 5:88; 20:81; 23:51

[60] Old Testament, Genesis 4:16-17
[61] Qur'an 3:26
[62] Old Testament, Genesis 17:4-5; Genesis 48:19
[63] Qur'an 29:45
[64] Qur'an 40:64; 64:3
[65] Qur'an 45:13
[66] Qur'an 3:96
[67] Ibid
[68] Qur'an 2:148-150
[69] Qur'an 2:213
[70] Qur'an 99:1-5
[71] Qur'an 3:110
[72] Old Testament, Numbers 22:28

4

Racism and Reconciliation

[73] Old Testament, Ezekiel 37:3-4
[74] Old Testament, Genesis 14:18
[75] Bible, Job 10:22
[76] Bible, Matthew 4:19; Mark 1:17
[77] Qur'an 3:64
[78] Dr. Margaret Mead (December 16, 1901-November 15, 1978) was one of America's most celebrated and well-known cultural anthropologists. One of her most famous quotes was: "Never doubt that a small group of thoughtful, committed citizens can change the world; indeed, it's the only thing that ever has".
[79] New Testament, John 9:5
[80] Qur'an 7:11; 40:64; 64:3
[81] Ibid
[82] Qur'an 2:148-9
[83] Ibid

[84] New Testament, John 12:32

[85] Qur'an 50:16

[86] Qur'an 26:75-8

[87] Qur'an 13:11

[88] New Testament, John 14:10-11

[89] Qur'an 18:110; 41:6

[90] New Testament, Luke 22:53

[91] Qur'an 18:47; 56:5; 20:105

[92] Qur'an 31:10

[93] Qur'an 35:12

[94] Sahih Bukhari, Volume 5, Book 58, Number 137: Narrated Anas bin Malik: The Prophet said to the Ansar, "After me, you will see others given preference to you; so be patient till you meet me and your promised place (of meeting) will be the Tank (i.e. Lake of Kauthar)."

[95] Qur'an 3:185; 21:35; 2957

[96] Old Testament, Genesis 3:4-5

[97] Ibid

[98] The song, *"How Sweet It Is (To Be Loved By You)"*, was initially recorded by soul artist, Marvin Gaye, in 1964 for Motown Records. It was written by the song writing team of Holland-Dozier-Holland. Other recording artists that covered this song: Jr. Walker and the All Stars (1966) and James Taylor (1975).

[99] Father Divine (1879-1965), was founder of the International Peace Missions Movement. He became famous during the Great Depression for his Peace Mission movement that drew thousands of disciples (white as well as black) at a time when nearly all the religious congregations in the United States were segregated.

[100] Noble Drew Ali (born Timothy Drew or Thomas Drew), January 8, 1886-July 20, 1929, was an African American religious leader who founded the Moorish Science Temple of America. He was considered, by his followers, to be a prophet and he founded a proto-Islamic movement in 1913 in Newark, New Jersey, before relocating to Chicago. Noble Drew Ali taught that African Americans were descendants of the Moors, but had lost this knowledge as a result of slavery in America. He preached black pride and advocated all African Americans to convert to Islam.

[101] Old Testament, Genesis 9:21-26

[102] New Testament, Matthew 24:37